101 *ways* to Have *True Love* in Your *Life*

DAPHNE ROSE KINGMA

CONARI PRESS

First published in 2006 by Conari Press,
an imprint of Red Wheel/Weiser, LLC
York Beach, ME
With offices at:
368 Congress Street
Boston, MA 02210
www.redwheelweiser.com

Library of Congress Cataloging-in-Publication Data
Kingma, Daphne Rose.
   101 ways to have true love in your life / Daphne Rose Kingma.
     p. cm.
   Includes bibliographical references and index.
   ISBN 1-57324-256-X (alk. paper)
     1. Love. I. Title: One hundred and one ways to have true love in your life.
     II. Title: One hundred one ways to have true love in your life. III. Title.
   BF575.L8K49652 2006
   152.4'1–dc22   2005017660

Typeset in New Baskerville by Suzanne Albertson
Printed in Canada
FR

13 12 11 10 09 08 07 06
 8 7 6 5 4 3 2 1

The paper used in this publication meets the minimum requirements of the American National Standard for Information Sciences—Permanence of Paper for Printed Library Materials Z39.48-1992 (R1997).

CONTENTS

The Gift and Practice of True Love

Love is the one thing that, invariably, people want more of in their lives. A lot of people want more money; a lot of people want more time, more peace, more friends, more fun, longer vacations, more radiant health, or a promotion at work; but just about everybody wants a true love.

We don't even know exactly what love is. We talk about it, long for it, fall apart when it goes away, and do just about anything to try and get it back; but no matter what our particular stance about it at any given moment, somewhere in our hearts we know that love is the most important thing in our lives.

Love is energy. It is the energy that is our very essence, an energy so glorious that when we're tapped into it, our feelings and our very lives are instantly transformed. We love to love, and to be in love; and our search for true love is one of our chief life's occupations. We're overwhelmed with the beauty of new romance, the solace of abiding love, the steadfast joy of deep friendship. We are always seeking love, because our search for love is our soul's reach for that sublime state in which our separateness is dissolved and we feel a profound and joy-filled sense of connection. That is precisely why so much of our lives is consumed by this undertaking. We know that love is the best we can ever experience, the highest we can be.

The discouraging part of our search is that sometimes it can feel as if love is the path of the angels and not of mere struggling mortals whose childhoods and daily experiences are so endlessly mundane as to make love seem endlessly elusive. Indeed, it is in the area of love and relationships, precisely, that most of us have received so little instruction. Instead, it's assumed that we all know how to love, how to get loved and how to keep love alive. As a consequence, we're not aware of the simple things we can do to nurture the heart and soul of our relationships. The great news is that no matter what your circumstances, you can learn to feel love and give love, to be loved and loving, and to draw the experience of true love into your life. As you do, your growing experience of love will transform your life and bring you increasingly into an awareness of your existence as a hauntingly beautiful gift.

Achieving true love, especially in the form of a particular person to love deeply and long, is a practice. Even if you aren't particularly gifted at it, you can learn how to love. Like the strength of your muscles or your singing voice, your capacity to love and to attract love can be developed. First of all, you need to know the attitudes and behaviors that can bring an outcome of love. Second, through the repeated enactment of these behaviors, you will see more and more love emerging in your life. Through the combination of learning and practice you can actually call more love into your life.

This book is a guide, a sampler, really, of 101 things you can do to bring true love into your life and to sustain it once it's arrived. The information will enhance your intention; but it is your enactment—your practice—that will make real love come alive. Study, and then act on these simple ways; and I promise you'll be the happier for it. Love will start to lead and follow you; and you will have a sense of the incredible beauty and preciousness of your life and of the gift of love that lies like a precious jewel in the midst of your relationships.

I wish you true love.

1

Loving Yourself

Love Yourself

*L*oving yourself is of the utmost importance. If you don't know how to love yourself, you won't know how or how well to treat others, and you may have problems with what we call boundaries. Instead of having clarity, you'll stumble through swamps of low self-esteem and thickets of self-loathing that will derail you in your efforts to "love others as yourself."

In order to love yourself, you must first understand that self-love isn't narcissism. Nor is it egotism, self-righteousness, excessive self-involvement, stubbornness, conceit, or greed, all of which have given real self-love a bad name. Rather, it is the solid internal grounding from which you can become your most authentic self.

Learning to love yourself is a process. For when you really learn to love yourself, you'll no longer have to work at it every minute. By continually reminding yourself of how important you are, how important loving yourself is, you will eventually arrive at the place where self-compassion comes almost automatically. From the steady practice of a gentle unconditional care of yourself, you will be able to reach out to others with exquisite generosity and a bounteous open heart.

In time you will see that self-love is also a spiritual matter. It's not just learning to treat yourself better, it's also learning to see and feel yourself as one of the threads in the vast human shawl, as deeply, indeed, unconditionally received by a caring and beautifully ordered universe. It is when you embrace this connection that you can truly love yourself. This true, felt sense of yourself as a precious part of the universe is really the ultimate source from which you can love others.

Begin this beautiful, powerful journey to yourself by taking a single step of caring for yourself today. For you, what would that step be? Write it down on a piece of paper. Paste it up on your bathroom mirror and then take it!

Value Your Uniqueness

When we come into life, our souls step out of the timeless eternal and into the finite moment of living as human beings. In this moment, and in the remarkable context of living on earth, we become both agents and receivers of the gifts of personality. We acquire that vast, amusing, unique, and frustrating array of attributes and attitudes, predilections and possibilities, from which we compose the symphonies of our individual lives. When it comes to personality, no human being is exactly like any other; and no matter how much you may share with, be influenced by, or bond with another, only you can be yourself.

It's a pleasure and a privilege to be yourself. In fact, just being born is a compliment. Having a chance to feel, see, and live your life, in precisely the way that only you will, is a sterling, never-to-come-again opportunity.

It's easy to forget this. We sometimes feel stranded, hemmed-in, and alone, not liking who we are, not being happy to be alive, disparaging our precious selves. But being yourself, living out your uniqueness, is precisely the beauty of being alive; when you ignore or forget to celebrate your uniqueness, you insult, in effect, the consciousness that gave you life.

And if you, who lives, breathes, suffers, and enacts all that is yours uniquely to experience, are unable to value all that you are, who can? And who will? Honoring you is your job. Nobody else can do it. Nobody else has the knowledge or experience. And nobody else should have to, for honoring yourself is your most important work. It is the ground of loving recognition from which your talent for honoring others will inevitably spring. To honor yourself is to know yourself in a truly valuing way. No other love you have or share or give will reach its full dimension until and unless you have first learned to truly honor yourself.

Practice Loving Yourself

I f you have trouble loving yourself, imagine that everyone in the world is a hungry soul whose life has been imperfect. Like you, they had imperfect parents. Like you, tragedies and difficulties befell them. If you could hear each person's story, you would probably be moved to tears and want to reach out and embrace that person. You would want to tell them that in spite of everything they've gone through, they have great value.

You might also want to thank them for having the courage to move from where they came from to where they are now, expressing your admiration of their goodness and beauty and uniqueness. You would want to tell them that, indeed, certainly, in the eyes of God and also in your eyes, there isn't any question that they deserve to be loved.

Imagine that all these beautiful souls are standing before you, waiting for your blessing. When you look in your heart and ask yourself whether or not you can unabashedly give it, your heart spills over with generosity and laughter and love. You can't imagine anything easier or more natural than loving each person for exactly who he or she is.

Now take a step toward loving yourself by imagining yourself at the head of the line of all these souls who are asking for your blessing, waiting for your approval, and see if you can't embrace yourself with the quiet heartfelt conviction of knowing that you're alright— that you're perfect—just as you are. As you do this, you will begin to feel deeply, in your own heart, the quiet, steadying gift of your own intelligent love. Loving yourself means that just as you're willing to rush to the aid of anyone else, you will rush to your own aid; you will come to your own rescue. You will acknowledge your talents, you will remember your own value, and you will know every minute that you deserve to live. Come on, take the first step toward loving yourself!

Challenge Your Self-Criticism

Self-criticism is speaking badly about yourself and, in general, evaluating yourself in a negative manner. It is beating yourself up verbally for the sheer knee-jerk habit and indulgence of it, just because it's familiar to pick on yourself and put yourself down. Through self-criticism, you look at yourself and find yourself somehow unacceptable, not worthy of your own love.

Do you say any of these terrible things to yourself? My nose is too big, too small, too crooked, too pointy. My eyes are too dark, too light, too close together, too far apart. I'm too fat. I'm too thin. I'm too ugly. Why did I wear that fancy blouse—too dressy! Why did I wear that plain old sweatshirt—too shabby! I'm too wishy-washy. I should have tried harder. I shouldn't have bothered. I shouldn't have said that. I should've said that instead. I should've been nicer. More aggressive. Less blunt. I wasted way too much money on that hotel room, house, car. I didn't invest nearly enough money on that motel room, cottage, bicycle. I should've asked that cute girl out on a date. I was a fool to love him in the first place. It was the biggest mistake of my life to marry her. I should've been more patient with my mother. I should not have gotten angry with my father. I should've blamed him more. I should've thanked him more. I should've forgiven him before he died.

Today, if you catch yourself in a moment of self-criticism, stop, breathe, and then say one beautiful, appreciating thing to yourself.

Stop the Self-Blame

*S*elf-blame is imagining—no, it's being absolutely sure—that whatever's gone wrong is your fault. It's choosing to blame yourself rather than the ordinary circumstances of life or the people who are actually at fault for whatever's gone awry. When your form of not loving yourself is self-blame, you tend to see every problem as somehow caused by you, and you beat yourself up for it.

Does this remind you of you? It's my fault my parents fought all the time—I wasn't a good daughter. It's my fault my child is sick—I didn't keep him away from that kid with the runny nose. It's my fault my husband is overweight—I don't cook him healthy meals. It's my fault my wife is unhappy—I don't earn enough money. It's my fault my favorite team didn't win—I didn't wear my rally cap. It's my fault that it snowed last night—I didn't pray to the sun gods. It'll be my fault if the house burns down—I don't check the electrical wiring weekly. It's my fault the economy crashed—I didn't manage my money well. It's my fault the ozone is depleted—I don't use the right hairspray.

You can always go on blaming yourself, but why not pause for a moment, and consciously remind yourself of one of your real achievements—big or small—and then write it down. This will help you move one—or a hundred—inches closer to loving and enjoying yourself.

Understand Why You Have
Trouble Loving Yourself

$\mathcal{D}$eep down, any feelings of unworthiness you may have are tied to your very sense of survival. That's because when you were very young, you were completely dependent on your adult caregivers for survival. Somewhere inside you know this. So, naturally, when you're a child you feel you'd better measure up ... or else. Psychologically, it works like this: If I'm a good and perfect child, my parents will love me. If they love me, they'll take care of me. If they take care of me, I'll survive and thrive and become all that I'm meant to be. On the other hand, if I'm not good enough, they won't love me, they won't take care of me, and I won't survive. I'll be so neglected, I'll die.

This fear of death is not an entirely irrational fear. For example, my friend Tom, the son of an alcoholic, was frequently beaten with any blunt object that was handy, and he legitimately felt that his life was in danger. And my friend Jane, who learned that her mother had tried to abort her, correctly sensed that at some point her mother had wished her dead.

Whether the danger is obvious, or merely implied, the bottom line of all this early experience is that, psychologically, we believe we have to be lovable in order to survive. That's how our sense of our own value becomes related to an unconscious fear of death. This is one of the reasons why, in adulthood, our own acts of not loving ourselves can feel so deeply violating. Each time we don't love ourselves, we are recreating the unloved feeling we had as children. This, in turn, makes us feel once again as if our very lives are in danger. On an unconscious level, we're afraid we might treat ourselves so badly that we will die from the lack of our own self-love, and indeed many un-self-loving behaviors are deeply destructive and do result in death.

Now that you understand this connection, will you start being kinder to yourself? What little or big thing can you do today to show that you love yourself? Go to the gym or take a healthy walk? Listen to some beautiful music? Look for a new, more fulfilling job?

Allow Your Needs to Be Your Guide

When you allow yourself to be guided by your needs, your needs become the path that can lead you to yourself—and also to your beloved. Conversely, denying your needs or endlessly serving others to the detriment of fulfilling your own needs are both ways of not discovering who you are and of not allowing yourself to be loved.

Not needing is an inauthentic state. It's a denial of your humanness. That's because one of our most basic human characteristics is that we are creatures of need. To deny this—by being brutally self-sufficient, by manipulating others into serving you, or by pretending to have transcended need—is a form of hypocrisy. No one who's alive on the planet—not even avatars or saints—has totally transcended need. To be human is to need; and to need is to be human.

We need food. We need loving arms. We need air and light and the sun and the glistening fine white shine of the moon. We need to be listened to, to be heard. We need empathy, to be feelingly felt with. We need work that is a true expression of our spirits. We need company, compatriots on the path. We need witness: friends and strangers to reflect to us who we are. We need success—at something. We need peace.

Our needs are like weeds that spring up between the rocks on our path—insistent, organic, demanding. They are the barest, boldest truths of ourselves, the essential grit at our core. But often we don't treat them as such. We tap them down, shut them up, and talk ourselves out of them; and by the time someone's ready to meet them in a relationship, we don't even know what they are.

The opposite of not knowing your needs is becoming conscious of them—discovering what they are and then finding the words to express them. As their size, shape, and content are all gradually revealed, you will gain a map of yourself. You will see who you are, what you really do need, and what joy it will give you to have your needs fulfilled.

So discover what you need; speak up about it; and be open to receive. For knowing what you need and asking for it—clearly, strongly, directly—is an act of personal strength. It will allow you to be honored through the meeting of your needs, and it will allow the person who loves you the joy of loving you well.

Use the Expression of Your Anger
As a Way to Love Yourself

Anger is a complicated emotion. It can go all the way from rip-roaring destructive rage to the firm and quiet expression of the fact that you are holding the emotional energy of anger about something that's been done to you. At its worst, anger is flying off the handle, blowing your stack, beating somebody up, being a raving, roaring maniac. These expressions of so-called anger represent the emotion of anger and the physical power of aggression combined, and they are immature and inappropriate forms of anger, unleashed primarily for the benefit of the person who's unleashing them.

But anger is also a beautiful emotion. It's the emotion of self-care and self-protection. It is the emotion by which you can tell others that you are a worthy, valuable human being. It's the way you can tell other people that they've gone too far, that they've crossed an invisible boundary they shouldn't have crossed if they want to remain in your good graces. It's the sword by which you can cut away behaviors that dishonor you, the emotion through which you can teach others how to treat you as well.

Because there's always a strong negative energy connected with anger, people generally don't like it when other people are angry at them. There's a certain threat embodied in the energy of anger, the sense when you're the recipient of it, that some negative effect could be unleashed in your direction. It is the presence of this potential threat which makes anger such a powerful emotion, and which also enables it to serve on behalf of your well-being. It takes a lot of energy to express anger; and it takes a lot of receptive strength and energy to be able to receive the anger that has been delivered.

Loving yourself by speaking your anger doesn't mean becoming a raving hysterical maniac and letting it all hang out. Healthy anger has four parts: determining exactly what you're angry about; expressing it strongly and clearly; elaborating, if you choose, about what it refers to in your larger life; and asking for what you want instead. By elaborating, I mean explaining why it is that this particular behavior has the power to affect you so deeply. For example, "I'm angry that for the third time this week you're late. It makes me feel as if you don't care about me. It reminds me of how I used to sit waiting on the curb after school for my father, who would often make me wait for hours, and one time completely forgot to pick me up."

Elaborating is important because it gives the other person an opportunity to see you in the context of your life experience, and not just in the moment of your irritation with them. It gives that person a chance to see what you've been through, and in doing so, to love you better. And it gives you an opportunity to love yourself better because when you see how the infraction of the moment is part of a long and knotted skein of infractions that have hurt your spirit over many years, you can decide to protest instead of getting hurt again. You'll feel better because you will have stood up for yourself, and they'll feel better because they'll have regained your love and restored the harmony between you.

I hope that understanding all this will help you to use your anger to honor, cherish, and protect yourself.

Take Action

Taking action is a very powerful way of loving yourself. In psychological terms, acting out isn't ordinarily thought of as being a good thing. It usually means that instead of behaving like a conscious, forthright human being and talking about what you need, feel, or want, you "act out," that is, perform despicable behaviors like egging someone's car windshield or beating someone up in a dark alley. In this view, acting out is a kind of immature emotional behavior through which you indirectly express your feelings through action instead of simply stating them. In psychological terms, this kind of acting out is "passive-aggressive" behavior.

In the cliché marital transaction, for example, the woman who doesn't want to have sex and creates a headache to avoid it is acting out to create the outcome she desires. Rather than telling her husband she isn't interested, she feigns a headache and gets what she wants. The use of an action—in this case, getting sick—to communicate something she doesn't have the courage to communicate in words is what constitutes passive-aggressive behavior. It's called passive because it isn't direct, and aggressive because it actually constitutes a kind of emotional violation of the person against whom it's directed. Rather than acting out in a positive sense, it's a subtle emotional assault.

But now I'm suggesting that you act out as a way of loving yourself. In this case, rather than "acting out" in the negative psychological sense, I'm suggesting that you take action on your own behalf, that you act, instead of contemplate, ponder, analyze, or dish to yourself or with friends about what you need, want, desire, and deserve. I'm suggesting that you move from thinking about what you might do, to actually doing it. That you move from talking about it—"I don't like the looks of my hair"—to doing something about it—getting a new haircut or dying your hair purple. The difference between these actions and what we usually think of as "acting out" is that these actions are conscious and positive, and you do them on your own behalf.

I'm using the term "acting out" because I'm not just telling you to act—to take an action. I'm encouraging you to act out. It's the *out* part that's significant. When you act, you simply perform an action. You take a notion out of your head and do something about it. But when you act out, you take actions that are out of the usual frame of reference for your behavior. In other words, you do something different, something you've never done before, something you might have never imagined yourself doing.

Understand Why Taking Action Is Difficult

Sometimes it's difficult to take the actions we need to take on our own behalf. That's because when we were children our actions were often suppressed. Out of their own fears, or out of a natural sense of protectiveness, your parents may have stifled your energy, your creativity, your passion (sexual or otherwise), your initiative, your strength. Don't do that, you'll make a mess. Don't try that, you'll get hurt. Don't do that, what will the neighbors think? Don't wear that outfit, everybody will think you're weird.

In fact, you may have been told that some of your actions were unacceptable. As a consequence, instead of developing courage and originality in your behavior, your actions may have become repetitive and unoriginal. In order to gain approval, to receive the love you thought you couldn't live without, you may have learned to draw your world of actions very small. Instead of being an expansive adventurer, ever on the journey of discovering the expressions that could define you to yourself (and in time become the vehicle through which you can give yourself to the world), you limit yourself to the actions that are known to gain acceptance.

So rather than wearing the chartreuse high heels and practicing singing in your bedroom, you learned to dress down and shut up. Or rather than becoming an actress, you became a secretary. Rather than taking a trip to India, you went to the mall. Rather than being a passionate lover, you lived in a passionless marriage for twenty-five years. One way or another, because of the content of your life theme, you learned to play safe, to contract, to limit your wholeness by living small, by living "according to the rules."

Given all this, it's hard to act out, and sometimes, rather than being inspired by expansiveness or a dream, the acting out that changes our lives is inspired by the constriction around us. This is true either when we do something our parents would never think of, or when our acting out takes a subdued direction because our parents made the world so unsafe and chaotic that, in reaction, we make our own worlds structured and calm.

Stephanie, whose socialite mother conducted numerous affairs in Stephanie's presence and right under her father's nose, acted out by not marrying the corporate lawyer of her mother's dreams, but rather a steady, good-hearted carpenter her mother would never approve of. When his parents insisted that Hank become a minister, he became a rock musician instead. When her mother said she'd better settle down and stay in her hometown, Sharon, the star of her high school drama department, took off for New York. One way or another, the atmosphere our parents create around us defines the nature of our actions. We're afraid to act, we react, or we act in a different way because of the role that action played in our relationships with them.

When I was in college, I used to ride the bus every day for an hour on my way to my job at the hospital. Day after day I'd see the same older woman riding on my bus. As time went by we gradually had an opportunity to speak. One day when we were sitting next to each other, a person sitting across from us was reading Life magazine and on the cover was a photograph of several famous mountain climbers. The woman noticed the picture and remarked that it reminded her of her son. "When he was a teenager he just loved to climb mountains," she told me. Then she went on to tell me a lot of other unusual things he'd done when he was a boy and young man. I remarked that with all those experiences, he must be having a very interesting life. When I said that, the woman paused for a moment, and her face grew still. Then she told me that her son had died in a mountain climbing accident. I told her I was so sorry. When she turned to thank me, she said, "Well, that was his way; I wasn't surprised. He died being himself." Then she told me she'd always found peace with his death because he'd died doing something he loved.

Despite her own loss, this mother had a great enough heart to encompass that it was in her son's nature to climb mountains. She didn't stifle him; she even had the expansiveness of spirit to recognize that even in his death he was being exactly who he was meant to be. She was that extraordinary parent who in fact supported her son's "acting out." How can you be that "parent" to yourself?

Clear Out What Doesn't Serve You

To clear out means both to remove and to make room for. In terms of loving yourself, clearing out is making a space of clarity for yourself. This is another very important way in which you can love yourself. When you clear out, you create a clearing for you—in your psyche, in your environment, in your brain, in your house, on your dance card, in your closet, on your kitchen table, in the clutter of your conscious mind, or in the dark rooms of your unconscious where you hold yourself in bad opinion. The term clearing itself is a very beautiful word. When you think of a clearing in nature, you think of a clearing in the forest, a beautiful space in which sunlight can fall, in which new things can grow.

If you've ever traveled in Germany, you may have noticed that among the soft rolling hills there are frequently tight-knit forests of tall, black trees. From time to time, you can also see a clearing in these forests, an open expanse of land where tree by tree the land has been cleared so that a village could be built or a beautiful vegetable garden planted. When I see these gentle spaces in the midst of the forests, I always contemplate the magnitude of energy, the many hours of sheer manpower, the number of saws and axes and horses and wagons that were required to make peace and space in the middle of these dense forests, the labor of love by which a clearing had been made.

If you really want to love yourself, it will be both good and necessary to make a clearing in the darkness of your inability to love yourself. Like the beautiful openness in the forests I traveled through, making a clearing is not an easy task. It requires energy and steadfastness and strength. It will require courage and intention. To clear out from your life what doesn't belong requires devotion, not only to the task—to the labor of clearing out—but also, and above all, to yourself.

Nourish Your Self-Concept

We all have some basic idea of who we are, what's good and bad about us, what we're total failures at, and what we've got a fairly good chance of achieving. Psychologists call this notion—and we all have one—our "self-concept." In a person who loves him or herself, this notion of who they are matches up pretty well with who they actually are and how other people see them. In people who have difficulty loving themselves, on the other hand, this picture is significantly distorted due to poor mental habits.

People who have difficulty loving themselves have a "poor self-concept." That is, they have one or several opinions about themselves which are inaccurate in a negative direction, and which, in spite of their desire to feel better about themselves, they unconsciously perpetuate. Even if you know you'd like to love yourself better, you may tell yourself many times a day, in a variety of ways, that you aren't good enough. The ways you communicate this may be spoken or internal statements you make about yourself. Or your poor self-concept may be demonstrated through such self-dishonoring behaviors as overeating, addictions, excessive television watching, or obsessive Internet surfing. With an incorrect self-concept, a person will say such things as "I can't do anything right, I'm hopeless, I'm fat" (when they're actually a good weight for their height) or "Nobody'll ever fall in love with me," when, in fact, they've already had a number of successful relationships.

The good news about your self-concept is that, even if you have a bad one, you can change it. Since it was developed over time, it can also be revised over time. In fact, you can purposely construct a healthier self-concept by clearing away the old messages and creating new ones.

You can begin the process by developing awareness. Start noticing how much negativity there is in how you currently think about yourself. Make a list of what you say or put a mark on a piece of paper each time you say something negative about yourself. Then, at the end of the day, tear it up. From now on, instead of indulging in these critical remarks, simply start saying to yourself that you're not going to listen to them anymore. It may seem strange to think that just telling yourself not to do something will work, but it will. In the same way you listened to all the negative things you said about yourself—and responded by building a negative self-concept—you can now begin to turn off these voices, and encourage a more self-affirming view of yourself to emerge. When all this negative self-talk is out of the way, the real you will have a chance to show itself.

You can speed up the development of your positive self-concept by creating what I call The Self-Concept Book. Here's how you do it: Buy a little book that attracts you, and from now on, each time someone says something complimentary about you, write it in your book. For example, if, in a passing conversation, someone says that you're a wonderful listener, that you're so funny, or that you have a wonderful smile, write it down. It may seem pedestrian, but the more you do this, the more your view of yourself will change. Instead of being cluttered with all the old messages about your inadequacies, your interior space will begin to fill with a positive awareness of who you are. You will begin to see your own value.

As you continue to write these things down, you'll also notice that all the people who observe you will tend to have a consistent response to who you are. A number of people will mention your beautiful smile, bunches of people will notice how funny you are, most of the people you know will mention your sparkling intellect or your great taste in clothes. Instead of feeling like the battered, tattered, inadequate person you used to think you were, you'll realize that there are beautiful, amusing, precious, and extraordinary things about you. A new picture of who you are will emerge, and this will be your self-concept. Are you ready to crumple up the paper with negative remarks? Go out and buy a beautiful self-concept book today.

Discover Your Gifts

A sad consequence of not loving yourself is not seeing the beauty and uniqueness of who you are. You can't see your gifts; you don't think about what you're here on the planet to do. Instead of living an inspired, fulfilled, contributing life, you're running around like a crumpled balloon trying to gather enough oomph just to carry on. When you love yourself, however, you can recognize and give your gifts. It's that simple. And it's very important. Because the world needs your gifts.

Right now, you may not have a clear sense of what your gifts are, but once you start loving yourself, you will begin to get a sense of them. They will show up in the places that used to be filled with negative remarks. You'll also begin to ask the questions of why you're here, and what you're supposed to be doing with your life. When you share your talents, you will feel fulfilled. Indeed, the more you love yourself, the more you'll begin to understand that you're not just here to feel great about yourself and your life, but you are also invited—indeed, required—to give your gifts, to use them. Giving and using your gifts will be part of your lifelong work of loving yourself.

What are your gifts? How might you use them?

2

Preparing for Love

View Yourself with Compassion

All of us know what a morbidly delicious temptation it can be to beat yourself up about almost anything that goes wrong in your relationship, or for that matter, in life in general.

If you don't have a fight, or if you're too chicken to pick a fight, if you have an orgasm or you don't, if it takes you forever to decide something or you decide impulsively, if you waste money or are a miser, if you're a neatness fanatic or a slob—whatever your habits, your way of doing things, you may be blaming yourself for whatever goes awry in your relationship.

Rob blamed himself for years, because whenever he and Jane had to make a decision about anything really important, he mulled it over for weeks. He analyzed it, slept on it, consulted with his, as he called them, "secret agents," then, long after Jane had made up her mind and was tap-tapping her pencil on the kitchen table in impatience, he'd finally make his decision.

Once "his stewing" as Jane referred to it meant that they lost their chance to buy what they both had thought was their dream house. Rob was so busy analyzing the comparables, checking out loans, that three weeks into his process the house was snapped up by somebody else. Although Jane was disappointed, she actually recovered fairly quickly. "These things happen," she said, "don't worry, we'll find another perfect house."

But long after they'd moved into a wonderful house, Rob was still beating himself up about the house his indecisiveness had lost. "I should have listened to Jane. I shouldn't be such a perfectionist about everything. Why can't I just make up my mind?"

The reality is that no matter your style, you're doing the best you can. Beating yourself up, blaming yourself, focusing endlessly on your faults—the way you might have been or should have been, done it or not done it—never improves the situation.

Look at yourself with compassion. Enjoy your curious little idiosyncrasies. Go easy on yourself. Acknowledge that it's just fine to be you. Let it be all right that you're different from everybody else. As the Yiddish adage asks, "If I be like him, then who will be like me?" So give yourself a break and decide that you're just fine exactly as you are.

Believe That True Love Awaits You

If you've been sitting around in the singles' department, watching the handsome guy at the pool, if you've been overwhelmed by a career that hasn't left time for intimacy, if all your friends are married and you feel like the only person in the world who hasn't found "the one," then you may believe that there won't ever be a true love for you.

If that's true, then you need to start believing that love does indeed await you. Just as nobody gets to Paris without believing that Paris exists, nobody falls in love without believing that a wonderful love is possible for them.

That's because conceptualization creates reality. In the story of almost every successful tycoon, we read that there was a belief that against all odds he or she would succeed some day. It's no different with you: what becomes manifest in your life arrives because consciously and unconsciously, you believe it can happen—whether it's a better job, a new car, or a true love.

The precondition of love's ever arriving is that you believe that somewhere out there is a real live person for you to love. If you believe it, it'll be true; if you don't, it will never happen. In fact, the person who could be the love of your life could step right up and look you in the eye, and you could say, "Excuse me, I've got an appointment," and head off in the opposite direction.

Believing that there's a true love for you may seem like a very small thing, but for a lot of people there's a great big hovering doubt that this wonderful thing called love could actually happen to them. Maybe you've already had twenty-four lousy relationships, maybe your fiancé died in a car crash, maybe you've always believed you aren't pretty enough, smart enough, or successful enough, or you're so shy that you can't even imagine having the kind of conversation that could get you into a relationship in the first place.

Remember Cinderella? She lay in rags on her pile of cinders and dusted up after her nasty stepmother and stepsisters. The furthest thing from her mind was that she, the raggedy cindersweeper, could ever fall in love.

Yet deep inside, Cinderella had faith, because when the Fairy Godmother showed up, she was open to the possibility that something good could happen to her; she didn't run away.

Instead, she put her faith in the Fairy Godmother, she accepted that the pumpkin turned into a coach, and she stepped into the little glass slippers with absolute confidence. She didn't say, "My goodness, how do you expect me to walk on these, they're going to splinter the minute I put my feet inside them?" No, she was open to love. Deep inside, she'd already said, "I believe in love; I believe that miracles can happen."

If you don't believe in Fairy Godmothers, you'll certainly never see one. And if you don't believe in love, it will never show up for you either. So take a risk, find the faith, open your heart, and believe that the love of your life awaits you.

Trust That There's a Person for You

Believing in love requires, first of all, that you believe there is such an energy as love in the world, and secondly that you believe that love in the form of an actual person will also be available to you. Love is a vast energy that's around us all the time. It's just looking for a way to be embodied in human form. But if you don't believe this energy exists, you'll certainly never experience your particular cupful of it. It will only be an idea.

If you say to yourself, "I know love is out there; I know it's the greatest power in the world, and I want my share of it," then a very beautiful thing will start to happen. You will start to encounter love on every corner, in the eyes of every person you meet, in poignant moments you share with strangers, in the sweetness you share with your friends. And if you ask for it specifically and believe it will come, you will also one day experience it in the form of a particular person with whom to fall in love.

Trusting that there's a person for you is more than having a vague, odd, floating notion that somewhere out there someone nice might exist. It means holding the powerful, beautifully honed conviction that a real person is available for you. The person of your dreams, the human being who is your excellent counterpart, the one who can actually nourish, excite, delight, and fulfill you, really does exist.

The difference between the kind of belief I'm talking about here and the sort of passive, half-hearted hope you might already have is that you are actually convinced in your heart that this wonderful thing can happen to you. If what you want is a real live human being to love, you really have to believe that there is such a person and that he or she is in just as much of a state of longing as you are. Rather than saying "Well, maybe someday someone will come along," which is a kind of giving up, you need to say, "I'm taking a stand that the person I can fall in love with actually exists and absolutely will show up in my life."

Many years ago I had a conversation with a woman who lived in the same apartment complex as I did when we both were young married women in Washington, D.C. One day, when we were having tea, she said, "I always used to be worried that I'd never fall in love and get married because I'm not pretty. But then, one day, in my mother's kitchen, I looked at all her old kettles and pans, and I realized that for every crooked pot there was a crooked lid. Right then I stopped worrying about whether I was pretty enough, because I knew that there was someone out there who would be just right for me, a person whose imperfections would be the perfect complement to mine."

I can still remember that just as she finished talking, her charming husband came home. Her belief, even in the face of what she knew to be her own limitations, was what allowed her to become available to love, and her availability is what allowed her husband to find her.

The same is true for you. For not only is there a crooked pot for every crooked lid, but there's also a king for every queen and a mirror for every face that chooses to look into it. There is a heart and a soul that is the counterpart to each heart and soul that is asking for love. So if you want to fall in love, believe in love, and surely it will come and find you.

Make Yourself Available

If you were ever a kid who walked up and down the street looking for a penny in the gutter, you know what it is to make yourself available for what seems to be impossible. People don't just leave money on the street for us to gather up in our hot little hands, but if you're a determined child and you walk around the block enough times, chances are you'll find that shiny penny.

Making yourself available to love is a lot like that. You have to present yourself at every opportunity and show up everywhere with every level of your being. The How-to-Snag-a-Man relationship books tell you that showing up consists of buying a great wardrobe, going to singles bars, placing personals ads, and engaging in all kinds of wily, seductive, and ultimately unauthentic behaviors that might get you to cross paths with someone who's just as inauthentically pursuing you. All these methods do, of course, increase your statistical possibilities of meeting someone to date or even marry you.

But if you've already done those things with less than fabulous success, and you'd like to meet a real person, who could deeply love the real you, that will require being truly available.

There's more to being available than having your body in a particular environment where somebody else's body might also simultaneously show up, or even your image on the internet where somebody else's virtual self can be reviewed by you. There's more to availability than having a hot outfit or being tall, dark, and handsome. In fact, the really significant aspects of being available are internal.

What I'm really talking about is a heart that is saying, "I'm ready,

I'm willing, I'm curious; I'm putting myself on the line at every level, to allow love into my life."

This is very different and much more subtle than buying a new dress and showing up at the party. It means you're aware of your inhibitions (I'm scared or I'm shy) and prohibitions (I'm too old or I've failed at love too many times), and that despite all your reasonable fears, you're still sending out the message, "Here I am, Love, come get me; I'm yours."

What does it take to be able to utter such optimistic statements? It takes being open. Openness refers to the way we approach the world, our circumstances, other human beings, and life itself. When it comes to taking the risk of being open, we have two choices. We can participate in life as if it were an insult or an assault, something we have to put up with, fight against, and protect ourselves from, or we can be receptive human beings who say, "I think there must be something purposeful and beautiful here, and I'm open to discovering what it is. I'm just one person, bumbling along on my life's little path, but I'm certainly willing to be surprised."

Being open is a stance of vulnerability. It is being available to the mysterious, being curious about the strange, and being willing to entertain the unexpected in every dimension.

For you, what specific actions would openness consist of? Are you willing to take the risk of being open?

Open Your Heart

If you really want to come into your life, you have to have an open heart. It isn't enough to be intellectually open, to say, "Well, I think love's a great idea, and if someone showed up, I'd certainly give some thought to falling in love." You need to be open with your emotions as well, and with your feelings and your attitudes.

Being emotionally open means you've consciously acknowledged that no matter what wounds you've already suffered (and we've all suffered more than it feels like we can bear), you're still willing to be open to love. It's like there's a little voice inside you saying, "I know my heart's been broken 50,000 times, but I still want the butterfly of love to fly down and sit on my shoulder. Besides, my broken heart is so strong from breaking all those times that it will just jump for joy when my true love arrives."

Being emotionally open isn't always easy. It's not a state you arrive at without any effort on your part. It takes work. It means that somewhere along the way you've faced head on (and worked through) the fact that your heart *has* been broken before, that you're tremendously vulnerable, that you do have doubts and fears, and that despite your fears, you're willing to try again.

In a larger sense, being openhearted indicates that you recognize yourself as an emotional being, and you're willing to experience your feelings. You realize that your emotions—joy, sorrow, fear, and anger—

are a constant undercurrent that moves through your body, and you are willing to feel all these feelings.

We all have this constant flow of feelings, but whether or not we're willing to experience them is what makes us open like flowers or close like tombs. Letting your feelings move through you keeps you emotionally flexible and up-to-date. Because you're not dragging along unresolved fears, anger, resentment, or sadness from the past, your heart is available to what's occurring now. So, when you meet someone who might be appropriate for you, you can bring yourself wholeheartedly to this new experience.

To see if your heart is open, ask yourself the following questions:

- Do I have a positive, curious, welcoming, trusting attitude about most human beings?

- Am I willing to work through the wounds of my childhood to open my heart to another person?

- Would I be willing to work through my memories of the heartbreak in my previous relationships in order to love again?

If not, make a pledge to yourself that you will ask each day for the resolution of these hurts. Seek outside help if you need to, because when you consciously ask for this healing, it will be forthcoming.

Come Out of Your Cave

*M*aking yourself available to a relationship often requires a change of behavior on your part. You have to go where love can find you. For example, if you've been hiding out, staying home every Friday night, watching TV and wishing you had a date, you might need to make yourself available by accepting that invitation to the neighbor's party. But true availability goes way beyond just showing up. So when you're at the party, all of you needs to show up: your words, your personality, your spirit. This means that you'll join the conversation even if you feel shy, speak even if you're not spoken to, express appreciation, admiration, curiosity. If someone inquires about who you are, asks why you're there, or what you want out of life, you cough up the truth—"I'm here because I've been hiding out for fifteen years and now I want a relationship"—instead of responding with some coy party jargon.

Making yourself available means that instead of being down in the dumps about your chances at love, you become ridiculously optimistic. Along these lines, I've always enjoyed the joke in which an old man stands on a corner day after day and every time a beautiful woman walks by he yells out to her, "Hey, will you come over here and give me a kiss?" Most of the women would walk right by and look insulted. Sometimes, the women would smile sort of pityingly, and every once in a dozen blue moons, a woman would actually come over and give the old guy a kiss.

Finally, a shopkeeper who had watched all this for several weeks came over and said, "Don't you realize what an idiot you look like asking all these women if they'd like to kiss you?" And the old man replied, "Well maybe that's true, but I'll bet I've had more beautiful women come over and kiss me than you ever have."

In his rather unconventional way, this man was making himself available. He was saying, "I'm standing out here on the corner, not just watching all the girls go by, but taking a risk of asking for what I really want. The odds are against it, but, by golly, every once in a while what I ask for actually happens."

As our man on the street demonstrates, if you have an optimistic attitude and make yourself available, your chances of getting what you want are immediately increased. In your own life, being available may run the gamut from going on the Sierra Club hike, even though you're falling-over exhausted after a 90-hour work week, to the spiritual brazenness of getting down on your hands and knees, shaking your fists at God and saying, "Send me someone right now, because I can't stand being alone for one more minute."

If you're staying home, watching TV alone every night, you're never going to meet anybody except the TV repairperson. That's why you really should put yourself in circumstances where people congregate— your church, your best friend's cousin's wedding reception. Go on all the blind dates that everybody sets up for you; join internet dating services, and even write the catchy, truthful, vulnerable personal ads that will capture some fine person's attention. Even if you get no immediate results, you will get some results. You'll have shown the cosmos what you want, and the cosmos will give it to you—sometimes in the most surprising way and sooner than you think.

Know Your Real Self

Knowing yourself is a tough task, and one that takes a lifetime. If you're looking for a relationship, there's a very specific kind of self-knowledge that's important. This kind of self-knowledge is making the effort to come into a deep awareness of your emotional being, who you truly are as a person. This includes having the courage to study your emotional makeup, to discover what hurts and delights you, what you're afraid of, what makes you happy, as well as identifying some of your main relationship needs.

You can begin this process of self-knowledge with something as simple as becoming aware of whether you're an introvert or an extrovert. Are you a person who likes to spend a lot of time sitting in the warm bath of your own quiet company, or are you someone who likes to be wildly expressive in a crowd? Are you a party person or a hermit?

Apart from being an introvert or an extrovert, what kind of lifestyle do you aspire to? Do you smoke or not? Drink alcohol or not? Are you a vegetarian? A movie fanatic? A couch potato or an exercise maniac? Do you need to spend time in nature? Listening to music? In meditation? Playing with your nephew? Visiting your parents?

It's important to know these things when you're looking for a mate so you don't present yourself with a kind of false advertising. We all have opportunities to meet people in circumstances that don't truly reflect who we are. The woman who meets her sweetheart at the office holiday party when he's wearing a suit—but he really hasn't been out of sweatpants for more than 24 hours in the last 20 years— is getting a false impression. She may think, "Ah, here at last is a man who can bring some class to my life," when the truth is he can't wait to get home and change back into his sweats. For this reason, it's worthwhile, as you're getting acquainted with someone, to reveal who you are in some of these seemingly trivial departments.

So know yourself and show yourself. What three things do you know about yourself that you would like the person who loves you to know? Which one of these three things are you ready to reveal today?

Get Clear About Why You Don't Have a Relationship

It may seem like a complete mystery that you don't have love in your life right now. But it's not. That's because underlying the presence or absence of a relationship in your life are some unconscious motivators that have helped to create the very situation you find yourself in.

You may be saying to yourself, "I want to fall in love; why doesn't somebody come along and sweep me off my feet?" You might think you're ready to fall in love, but the truth is, other forces that you may not be consciously aware of are also operating. When you bring these factors into conscious awareness, you can see how you may have been inhibiting yourself from finding love. By bringing these issues to light, you become able to meet the person you will love to love.

Indeed, the reason you're not in a relationship right now consists of a number of factors both within and outside of your control. Among the ones you can affect are the psychological and circumstantial reasons hidden in the veiled chambers of your clever unconscious. The reasons you may have for not being in the kind of relationship you say you want include relationship ambivalence, circumstantial conflicts, an incomplete recovery from a previous relationship, and the fear of facing your deepest fears.

If you're not in the ideal relationship, you might ask yourself the following questions. Is your desire for a relationship in conflict with your independence? (Ambivalence.) Are you too busy starting a career to spend time getting to know someone? (Circumstantial conflicts.) Are you still broken-hearted over the ex? (Unresolved previous relationships.)

Be Realistic About What Love Is

Trusting in love—that it will arrive and be right for you—creates a comforting nest where you can rest your faith, so you can take the risk of taking a look at your hopes with a cool, clear eye. When you're realistic—facing the truth about situations, people, and things—you're honoring yourself. Instead of fooling yourself with out-of-reach expectations, you're taking care of yourself by asking for something that can actually come to pass.

Being realistic is a unique form of trust, because it asks that you be responsible. It asks you to use the left brain—intellect, awareness, evaluation—as well as the right—intuition, feeling, impulse—to protect you from just foolishly, irresponsibly falling into the kind of relationship that could be like taking a dive at the sidewalk. To be realistic about falling in love, you need to understand what a loving relationship is. A lot of people who are looking for love have such wildly unrealistic expectations that the relationships they imagine couldn't possibly occur. That's why they're constantly disappointed. They don't trust in love and they shouldn't, because they're asking for the moon.

A real experience of love, on the other hand, is both grand and simple. At its grandest, it contains all our most romantic ideals, and at its most elementary, it is the simple joy of having another person with whom to share life's journey. In the form of an intimate relationship, love is both queenly and like a peasant girl, magnificent and very sweetly ordinary. It includes both the grand expanses of discovery and the ordinary pathways of daily life.

Since a relationship is an experience of trading feelings to a high degree, of being emotionally open and allowing another person's emotional reality to enter into yours, there's always an exchange through which you can both develop. It's the arena in which you can share your successes and woes, look for comfort and support, talk about the little irritating and huge overwhelming things that confront you day by day. It is this emotional connection that allows you to feel bonded to another human being and, because of this connection, also to become most yourself.

Indeed, the greatest gift of an intimate relationship is that it can give you *you*. It's an opportunity to discover yourself in the presence of the reflecting emotions of another person. In the mirroring of another person's awareness and, at times, through his or her frustrating lack of awareness, you will come to see yourself. It is in this intimate human context that you begin to discover what you really do feel, what's important to you, what delights you, what has troubled you always, and what's troubling you now.

A relationship is also a fine opportunity to apprehend another human being. It's a chance to really know another person in the round—not according to your preconceptions, your dreams about who that person might be, but of really discovering, as you might discover an incredibly beautiful landscape or an ancient sacred ruin, the remarkable mystery and beauty of another human being.

Relationships are also the way love teaches us what it is to be human. We learn this not only through our own feelings as they are endlessly evoked by our partners, but also through our direct experience of another person's uniqueness as it is endlessly revealed to us. Expecting this, working toward this, is being realistic about love.

Get Real About What You Want
Out of a Relationship

*S*ometimes it's easy to fantasize that just being married or in a relationship will make you happy and solve all your problems. This if-I-could-only-fall-in-love-then-everything-would-be-all-right kind of thinking falls into what I call the relationship daydreaming category.

Relationship daydreaming is the antithesis of relationship realism. Finding the love of your life is a serious undertaking, while relationship daydreaming is a form of emotional sloppiness. Because fantasizing is vague, it's likely you won't get results. In love, as in anything else we ask for, specificity brings results. The cosmos can respond only when you send out a message loud and clear. If you need a new apartment, for example, you need to specify, I need a new apartment in Cleveland. Or, I need an apartment with northern light so I can work on my paintings. Or, I need an apartment where the rent's no more than $900 a month—that's all my budget can handle.

If you don't know precisely what you want, you won't get it. When it comes to falling in love, fuzziness of desire can cause you to drag out an unsatisfactory relationship, or to suffer by yourself so long that you miss out on the very relationship that might be perfect for you. While a relationship isn't a panacea and certainly can't fulfill all your dreams, a good relationship does have certain characteristics that can make it not only suitable, but truly wonderful for you. So get specific.

For starters, look at the activities you'd like to enjoy with the person of your dreams. The reason this is so important is that, although you may not be thinking about it while you're feeling desperate, lonely, and miserable, when you're in a relationship, your experience will be comprised of all the things you either do or don't do with your partner. In their desperation to find someone to love, a lot of people overlook the vast areas of compatibility a relationship is actually made of and go for unions with totally incompatible people.

We all have a vast array of activities that are meaningful to us. Some are things we prefer to do on our own; others we like to share with someone. Bringing these two strands of preference into awareness is a major task of the realism of love, because when we fall in love we often mistakenly assume that we should want to share every moment and every experience with our partner, that "being together" is all we desire.

If you make this mistake, it can often backfire later, as, within the matrix of your relationship, you must once again discover the people and experiences that nurture your individual spirit. In truth, we're all much more particular than the "whatever-he-likes, whatever-she-wants" state of mind. What's most important is the "what-you-want" state of mind.

Know That Your Soul
Will Recognize Your Beloved

In the dating game, people can spend an incredibly long time trying to figure out if the person who shows up is "the one," whether he or she is the real turtle soup or merely the mock. Being able to recognize "the one" doesn't have to do with whether he or she showed up with the right props—46 diamonds or a big fancy car. Rather, it has to do with your capacity for self-awareness, as well as your ability to assess another person accurately. This awareness of self and others has to do with your activity preferences, the thing you absolutely can't live without in a partner, and your negotiable desires.

But this kind of assessment of yourself and another can take you only so far because these characteristics operate at the level of personality, and we are also spiritual beings. We have morals, values, and an intuitive sense of the meaningfulness of our lives. So when it's time to choose "the one," these deeper levels of your being will also be operating. Your soul as well as your personality will have to be satisfied by your choice.

What is your soul aware of as the purpose of your life? What are the values you would stake your life on? When you're choosing a partner, be sure that these qualities are present in your partnership.

Discover Your Activity Preferences

*L*earning your own preferences will allow you to present yourself clearly and help you to evaluate the person who's presenting him or herself to you. Compatibility in terms of shared activities and alone/togetherness time are important components of any relationship. You can avoid a lot of missteps and disappointments, crossed wires and crabbiness if, at the outset, you can communicate your real preferences.

If you're contemplating a new relationship, you should become aware of all the things that you like to do, both with a partner and by yourself. First, make a list of all the things you like to do. For example, make love, go to the movies, cook a gourmet dinner, go river rafting, do yoga, read a book, read twenty books, make beer, meditate, go to the gym.

Then put a "2" beside each item on the list that you'd like to do with a sweetheart and a put a "1" beside each item that you'd prefer to do alone. Afterwards, put your list away for a week. When you look at it later with fresh eyes, what does it tell you about what you're looking for in a relationship? Your list will show you the activities you like to share (and therefore the kind of relationship you'd prefer). It will also reveal the pockets of privacy you still want to preserve.

Of course, some of the things on your list may change with time, or with a specific partner. You may have wanted to go dancing with someone in the past whereas you may not enjoy dancing with a particular partner now, because you'd rather go to art galleries with her—or you may be tired of dancing altogether.

When you start a new relationship, don't ignore your list. It's a reflection of who you are, and you shouldn't abandon it no matter how much "in love" you may think you are. If your list says you like to go hiking alone—it's your meditation, your time for unwinding and communing with nature—but the woman you're dating says she wants to go hiking with you, then you've got a problem. Maybe it's a problem that can be negotiated, but it's certainly one that needs to be addressed.

If you're the world's coldest person who wears socks even in the tropics, and the man who's courting you wants to spend his whole life on the ski slopes with the woman of his dreams, then, ditto, you also have a problem. If your list says you love to socialize, to do business with a vivacious woman at your side, and you're dating a bookworm who doesn't even own a black dress, you've got a Grand Canyon of discrepancies to handle.

Conversely, if you like to work in the garden with someone and he does too, if you like to raise flowers and she loves to arrange them, if you both love to go sailing or shopping in Paris, then you're in the happy land of some instant compatibilities.

Whatever your list, trust it. Use it as a guideline. It may seem simple or even foolish, but as time goes on, you'll find that sharing what you love to share while having the solitude you need is extremely important.

Be Grateful for What Is

ratefulness is living in a state of great fullness in every dimension. When we inhabit this state, no matter what's going on in our lives, we feel that our hearts are full, our eyes are full of beauty, our ears are full of sounds that enthrall and delight us, and our consciousness is full of a fine awareness of the majesty of life.

If you're reading this book because you don't have someone to love right now, you may think you don't have a thing to be grateful for. "How can I possibly be thankful when the only thing I want I don't have?" you might ask. "Gratitude! What are you talking about?"

That's because gratitude usually seems like an emotion that comes after the fact of some experience. When someone gives you a beautiful gift, you are subsequently grateful. When you are taken out to a lovely dinner, you are appreciative afterwards. But in order to prepare for love, you must live in gratitude as a state of anticipation—not as the consequence of already having received something.

This defies our normal sense of the order of things. But when it comes to love, gratefulness is imperative. That's because gratitude is a magnet. It draws toward itself what is similar to it; it attracts what is resoundingly synchronous with it.

In other words, the joyful, thankful heart attracts a person who is also joyful and thankful. The woman who lives in a state of appreciation of life itself will draw into her circle the man who not only gives thanks for his life, but who will also appreciate her. The man who is thankful even in difficult circumstances will draw in a woman whose similar spirit of gratitude will make his life graceful with ease.

When we're not grateful, we reap the rewards of ingratitude: stinginess, poverty, lack, discomfort, confusion, difficulty. As we express our feelings in these negative modes, people who operate on these same impoverished wavelengths will join us in a chorus of whining and complaining. Difficulties will be drawn to us, because our consciousness is like a picnic ground where these energies can sit down and feast.

Conversely, when we live in a state of gratitude, all that is gracious, beautiful, and full of joy will come to us easily. It's interesting to note how so many of these positive words are full of fullness: beautiful, grateful, wonderful, joyful. When we hold these abundant attitudes, when we live in this state of being, our lives will be filled with what we have already adopted as the attitude of our hearts.

That's why it's important to look at every experience of your life—even the difficult ones—as something to be grateful for, because each has offered a gift or a teaching. So if you've had a great relationship, kick up your heels and say hallelujah, and if you have had difficult relationships, be grateful for all the things they have taught you.

Let every event be an instructor in your school of gratitude. For gratitude, more than any other state of consciousness you can adopt, is the attribute that can develop your capacity for love. And your capacity for love is, above all, the thing that will draw love toward you.

3

Living Your Love

Keep On Loving Yourself

All too many of us think love is the miracle by which, finally, we will become complete human beings. This is the fixer-upper notion of love, the idea that we're not all right as we are, but if we can just get loved by somebody, then that will prove we're ok.

Ironically, however, in order to be well loved, you need first to love yourself. For in love, we get not necessarily what we deserve, but what we *think* we deserve. Just as Harry Homemaker who has a house that's worth one million dollars might sell it for only $500,000 if that's all he thinks it's worth, so the person who underestimates his or her own value will always be shortchanged in love.

Love begets love. If you don't think well of yourself, you can't be positively affected by the person who is celebrating you for the specialness you don't believe you have. If you don't know, and love, what's important, special, precious, and beautiful about yourself, you can be sure you will not be serenaded, sent roses, lauded, paraded, or daily smothered in kisses by someone who does.

Loving yourself is knowing yourself, enjoying and valuing yourself, and understanding that self-knowledge is a lifelong personal enterprise. It means that you appreciate yourself at least as much as you value your honey, that you know he or she is as lucky in love as you believe you are. It means you measure your strengths and weaknesses neither with the abuse of self-deprecation nor the insanity of ego mania, but with genuineness, with accuracy. Loving yourself is acknowledging your flaws, and forgiving yourself for them. Loving yourself is reaching for more, for the best, in yourself.

When we put up with shabby treatment in love it's because we believe we don't deserve better. But self-love is always the model for the love you may reasonably expect, the true measure of the love you will give and get. Your heart can only hold as much love as you believe it can. So treat yourself better, believe you deserve to be treated well, and you will get treated even better in all the relationships you have.

Surrender Your Expectations

We usually get into relationships seeing their obvious possibilities, imagining specified outcomes, cocooning them with our own expectations. But what actually occurs is often shockingly different from what we expected. The person you wanted to marry has a phobia about commitment. The woman you knew would make a great mother decides to go off to law school. The suitor with the bottomless trust fund decides to give away all his money and live in a cave. Surprising revisions can happen on even the simplest levels: "When I fell in love with him, he was wearing a blue cashmere blazer and gray flannel slacks; but after I married him, all he would wear was sweatshirts and blue jeans."

Expectations come in two forms: general and specific. General expectations have to do with our dreams and plans for a specific relationship—that it will lead to marriage, that it will bring you children, that it will make you "happy." Specific expectations have to do with what we think we can count on day to day—he'll take out the trash, she'll handle the kids in a way I approve of. On one level, these expectations are all quite reasonable; it's appropriate to have long-range plans and goals, and it's legitimate to expect specific kinds of participation from your partner.

But when your relationship becomes a litany of failed expectations—what you hoped for but didn't get—it's time to look at what's happening from an entirely different perspective. Perhaps, instead of needing to "communicate better" or "negotiate your differences" on an emotional level, you're being asked, on a spiritual level, to learn to accept what is.

Accepting—finding a way to be comfortable with things as they are—is actually a very developed spiritual state. It means that you've relinquished the preconceptions of your ego and surrendered to what's been given to you. Maybe he's not the provider you hoped for, but his spiritual strength is a constant inspiration; perhaps she's not the housekeeper you wanted, but the way she nurtures your children is absolutely beautiful.

Acceptance allows your spirit to grow. When you're able to recognize the little miracles and great lessons that replaced your expectations, you suddenly discover that what you hoped for was pitifully puny compared to what was actually held in store for you and that, in a way far more complex and elegant than you yourself could have imagined, your life is following a sacred design.

So if you want a life that is larger than life and a relationship that is finer than your wildest hopes, peel back your expectations and surrender to what is.

Remember That Everybody Has Circumstances

In love we often expect our partners to do, stop doing, be, say, give, or receive whatever we want them to without remembering that they have lives of their own. Unfortunately (and fortunately) a relationship isn't a free-for-all for the indulgence by the other person of every one of our needs and whims. That's because everybody has circumstances, pragmatic realities he or she is caught up in, shaped by, and trying to manage. This means that the person you love won't always be available to love you precisely as you want.

At times your own circumstances can seem so overwhelming—being stuck for years in a dead-end job to put the kids through college; having to cope with an aging mother who has Alzheimer's; trying to get a degree while working full-time—that you can forget that your partner has circumstances too. Because life can be difficult, we often just want to be relieved, even saved, from our own difficult circumstances by the person we love. Why can't he just get us out of debt? Why won't she have sex with me whenever I want it?

Holding these hopes, though, is a way of ignoring one of the basic facts of life, which is that life isn't fair. We all have enormous burdens and chances are that your sweetheart, just like you, is trying to cope with more things than he or she would like to.

Unfortunately, it's all too easy to forget about another person's circumstances when we're at the effect of our own. I have a friend who used to pick endless fights with her husband because he never got home until after 8 p.m. Finally one night he said to her, "Do you think I *want* to work so late every night? I hate my job! But between sending you to nursing school and supporting three kids, I can't afford to quit." When she realized that he was as much a victim of circumstance as she was, she stopped complaining and instead starting giving him empathy and encouragement. Interestingly enough, not long after, he found ways to come home earlier most nights.

Remembering that everybody has circumstances is a way we join one another in the human condition. When we acknowledge in our hearts, and through our actions, that the other person, too, is at the effect of life's slings and arrows, we create a deeper form of bonding. Instead of being at odds, we see that we're all in this together. We recognize that we neither live, love, labor, nor suffer alone.

Practice the Art of Empathy

Feeling with and for someone—having empathy—is the deepest form of emotional participation that you can have with the person you love. In your intimate relationship it can make you feel more known and knowing, more fully recognized and seen, more beautifully and deeply connected.

Having empathy isn't necessarily easy. Indeed, of all the emotional interventions, empathy is the most demanding. For, to actually be able to enter into another person's experience so fully that she is able to feel your presence there with her is the embodiment of the highest degree of emotional refinement. To truly join your beloved—in the place of his powerlessness, or of her shame—is to have already, in some sense, visited these hellish realms on your own.

The supporting cradle of empathy is constructed from the huge array of feelings we have already felt in our own hearts and bodies. If you haven't first felt a particular feeling, or if you're unwilling to revisit it, your capacity to feel with another will be fuzzy, halfhearted, and dull.

Your empathy will be a feeble attempt at sharing the feeling, but not a truly empathic experience. That's why empathy is such hard work. You have to do your own work first, to acquaint yourself, in depth, with your own emotions. Only then will you have an Encyclopedia Britannica of the human feelings to refer to; because you have felt, you will "know what it feels like." You'll have a reference in your own body, an idea in your own mind, of what a particular experience is likely to feel to another person. Since you've "been there," you can truly empathize and create a powerful sense of communion.

Celebrate the Exceptional

ompliments are verbal nourishment. They generate self-esteem and in a very subtle way create a person in the full spectrum of his or her essence. Compliments invite the person who is complimented to embrace a new perception of him- or herself. Just as layers of nacre form a pearl over a grain of sand, so compliments collect around us, developing us in all our beauty.

Celebrating the exceptional will make you aware not only of the value of the other person but also of your own specialness. To contemplate the uniqueness of your mate is, at the same time, to inform yourself about your own fine qualities. For the exceptionalness of your beloved is a reflection of you; you would not be in the arms of this incredible person if there weren't also something very special about you. To honor your wife's beauty is to be reminded of your own worthiness. To relish your husband's sensitivity is to be aware that you are the kind of person in whose presence such emotional elegance can flourish.

In such ways do we confirm that we are not only lucky in love but worthy of being loved. To see the appropriateness of your being together is to have a sense of hope and joy about your mutual love. Therefore, lavish praise on the person you love, and the blessings will come back to you a thousandfold.

Shower Each Other with Kisses

A relationship needs to be S.W.A.K. Ever write that on the back of a letter? It meant that your letter was special because you sealed it with a kiss. Even when the courtship is over, your love needs to be sealed and affirmed with a multitude of kisses. That's because kisses are the sign, more than anything else, that we like, love, cherish, and adore the person we are kissing.

Kisses can carry all our little (and big and magnificent) messages of love. They're the sweetest, simplest, most common-denominator expression of your love; and whenever you give them, you nurture your bond.

Kisses also have a multitude of meanings. They're the sign that a new romance is beginning; they're the glue of affection, the counterpoint to passion. Wordless, they can say anything from "Honey, I'm home," to "Congratulations," to "I'm wild about you; you're the one I desire." Or, on the other hand, they can express a simple, "I'm sorry."

Just as kisses are the portal to erotic life in a new romance, they're the life support system of erotic passion in long-time love. They are the signature of passionate contact, the way we say we'd like to make love. But kisses aren't just the key-card to erotic passion. Once having entered the realm of sexual intimacy, they have a power and beauty all their own. They sweeten and deepen the sexual encounter, make it more playful or tender, more full of feeling.

Kisses lift the level of our experience from the daily and banal to the delicious and extraordinary. Kisses are the food of love.

Cuddle Up

The trouble with life is that it isn't cozy enough. In the baby part of ourselves, which every one of us still has, we all need to be hugged and cuddled, to be sweetly curled up with and kissed, to be lovingly and tenderly held.

Cuddling is nurturing of the body and the spirit and we all profoundly need it. To be touched and held, to have our skin—that miraculous fine thin silken wrapper of our being—caressed, addressed, remembered, and cherished, is one of the greatest human requirements. It's a leftover need from childhood, when most of us didn't get cuddled enough, didn't get held, or kissed, or dearly nestled nearly enough. That's why, now, we need to cuddle up, why we long to feel the gigantic embrace that grown-up cuddling is. We want to feel protected and safe. We want to feel nurtured and loved. We want to feel that there's more to life that just our chores and our work. We want to believe that having a body in a world full of bodies isn't a sad, lonely joke. Cuddling, therefore, being cozily with—on the couch, in the bed, in the kitchen, in the car and at the beach, in restaurants and subways, during the credits at the movies and in long lines at the bank—is an unadulterated pleasure that fills a giant human need.

Cuddling isn't a stand-in for any other thing—like sex, or a great conversation, or a night out on the town, or a trip to the lake, or your favorite baseball game. Cuddling is wonderful, helpful, healing, delicious, delightful, soothing, yummy, cuddly, and scrumptious all by itself. So cuddle up!

Do the Extraordinary Ordinary Thing

Part of the graciousness of love is that it allows us to deepen the meaning of even the simplest gestures of ordinary life, to make the commonplace uncommon, to make the familiar magic. Doing the extraordinary ordinary thing is performing a commonplace service for no reason, and in these days of instant everything, the formerly ordinary has become extraordinarily special. It's a luxury to have a homemade pie or a hand-mended sock.

From time to time, my cousin Jed gives his girlfriend Diane an envelope full of coupons, certificates in exchange for which he'll polish her shoes, sharpen the knives, plant the petunias in pots on the porch, and clean the ridiculously messy front hall closet. My friend Joanne mends her husband Steven's sweaters and sews all his missing buttons on. "It's the most special thing," Steven says, "so loving, because I know she doesn't really have the time."

Sometimes doing the extraordinary ordinary thing is simply creating an occasion to do some banal thing together. Whenever they have a dinner party, my friends Belinda and Jim wash dishes together, even though they have a dishwasher. "We really enjoy it. There's something about the warm soapy water and the linen dish towels that makes everything seem easy. For us, it's a time to decompress, to talk about the people at the party, how we compare with our friends, to remind ourselves of what we have. Some really quite amazing things come out. Normally, we'd never take the time to say the things we say in these dishwashing gabs, but there's something so safe about just standing there together at the sink, letting our hair down."

By doing the extraordinary ordinary thing you communicate in a very simple way that you love one another. You remind yourselves that you have thrown your lot together, that you want to keep you life knitted up together for the long skein of the future. And since ordinary things refer in our unconscious to uncomplicated times, they're therefore a wonderful balm to over-stressed lives. They remind us that no matter how complicated life can get, some of the sweetest, most solacing gestures of love are really very simple.

Take Care of Your Body

We often think of our bodies as our own private possession, and, of course, in a fundamental way, they are. But when you're in a relationship, your body is also the medium of your connection to your beloved. If you didn't have a body, you wouldn't be here to love anyone in the first place; and it is your body, your physical presence, with which the person you love is continually engaging. After all, it's your body you bring home from work every day; it's your body that sleeps with your darling at night. You have to look in the mirror to actually see how you look; but the person who loves you has to look at you all the time. When you're exhausted or depressed, your darling will see the weariness in your face and your stance, just as he or she will also recognize your sense of well-being, vitality, and happiness.

Because of this, the way you treat your body carries great significance in any relationship. It can be a gift, an asset, a joy, a grand celebration for your beloved, or a detriment, a burden, the occasion for a spiritual test. Just as radiant health and well-being can present beauty and inspiration to the person you love, so physical self-abuse or neglect can become the reason why your relationship starts to break down. If you don't take care of your body, you're sending a message to both yourself and your beloved—that you're not important to yourself, that he or she isn't very important to you either. That's because how you take care of your body is a reflection not only of how you feel about yourself but also of how you expect your sweetheart to feel about you. If you're in the process of destroying your body in one way or another (by smoking, drinking to excess, being a workaholic or a sugar, caffeine, sit-down-at-the-desk-and-never-get-any-exercise addict), how can you reasonably expect the person you love to delight in and enjoy your body or to reflect to you the love you haven't been able to give to yourself?

In sharing your body with the person you love, you are sharing your true essence. So honor that essence, the highest human expression of your embodied soul: by nourishing, loving, and cherishing your body—for yourself and for your beloved.

Keep In Touch

In these days of busy and complex schedules, it is actually possible to lose touch with the person you love, sometimes for days at a time. That's why we need to make an effort to keep an eye not only on our obligations and plans but also on our intimate relationships.

Keeping in touch means that you will keep your partner thoughtfully apprised of your life and times—your schedule and obligations as well as variations in routines and plans. There's nothing worse, for example, than having a sick child and being unable to track down your mate. Or being told he'll arrive at six that evening, only to have him show up two hours later. Emergencies and exceptions do come up, but having the commitment to fill one another in as much as possible, as soon as possible, will give your honey the resilience to withstand the irritating exceptions.

But keeping in touch should be more than merely an exchange of scheduling information. It also means that you'll find ways to communicate your love on a regular basis, regardless of how busy you are. One couple I know keeps a book on the living room table. When either of them has to be gone, he or she never goes away without leaving a message of love for the other person. They've been married eight years and the book is now the heartfelt tracing of a daily life lived out in thoughtfulness and love.

What can you do to make sure you're keeping in touch in your own relationship? What would you like your partner to do to keep more in touch with you?

Offer Your Help

We're all sufficiently busy with the things we do for ourselves and our jobs, spouses, and children, that we don't necessarily have time to do anything extra. That's why offering your help is a gift, a form of emotional generosity that can add a special grace to your relationship.

Offering to help is more than just being willing to divide up the burden of the chores. It's a way of saying that, for no reason other than love, you're willing to enter your sweetheart's world and bring some assistance to it. Help can come in many forms. It can be verbal solace (telling your honey everything is going to be all right), physical deliverance (lending a hand with the dishes), emotional comfort (listening to your sweetheart's woes), and a kind of jack-of-all-trades willingness to do whatever is needed ("Is there anything at all that I can do for you?").

This loving awareness says that, minute by minute, you notice what's going on with the person you love and are willing to participate in his or her circumstances even at a very mundane level.

This will endear you to your beloved because, in a multitude of tiny, subliminal ways, he or she will know you're paying attention and that you care. Offering to help is a simple way to affirm your connection and nourish your love.

Console One Another

*M*ore than we like to acknowledge, life is infused with tragedy. Everybody is given burdens of heart that are almost too much to bear. We all have sorrows and heartaches that bring us into landscapes of pain that seem almost untraversable. There are times when we feel that what we are experiencing will utterly destroy us.

To be aware of all this is to know how great our need is for consolation. Faced with the magnitude of the tragic in our midst, we can do nothing but attempt to extend the healing gift even if we feel totally unequipped to offer it. For no matter how inadequate our unpracticed gestures may seem, they will surely reach into the place that is aching for solace.

We all need to act as physicians of the spirit for one another. When we are assaulted by life's sorrows we need to feel the presence of the person who loves us. When we are broken-hearted we most need to be ministered to, and when we are in grief we need to be taken into the arms of love.

To console is to comfort—with your words, with your hands, with your heart, with your prayers. To console is to feel with one another, and thereby to divide the power of the loss. When you console, you listen from the innermost place in yourself, and make yourself and the person you love less alone.

Remember That Your Sweetheart Isn't Psychic

f I had a dollar for every time somebody said to me: "But why do I have to ask? He should know what I feel/want/think," I could give King Midas a run for his money and live in a castle built of gold bricks.

Love does a great many magical things, but it doesn't turn us into psychic wizards. We need to tell each other what we want and ask for what we need. And I mean *tell* and *ask*. If nothing but the blue angora sweater will do for your thirtieth birthday, *say* that or you may end up with a set of kitchen canisters. If you want your darling to wear the black silk strapless dress to the office Christmas party, *tell* her or she might just show up in that flowery number you hate. Not because he or she doesn't love you, but because he or she isn't psychic.

Wanting your sweetheart to be psychic is a wonderful fantasy. It would be great if he or she knew everything you wanted and could make it magically appear. Letting go of the dream that your honey will "just know" is really letting go of the childhood fantasy that your parents would always know exactly what you wanted. It's sad to think that love has limits, that getting what we want takes effort, but it does.

And once you've mourned your fantasy, remembering that your sweetheart isn't psychic will encourage you to be more forthright and adventurous in expressing your needs and desires, which will make it more likely that the other person will meet them. Receiving what you want will make your heart soft and happy and open. You'll feel more loving and more love will start flowing back to you.

Don't Mistake Your Sweetheart For Yourself

It may seem absurdly obvious that your sweetheart isn't you, but one of the worst mistakes you can make in love is to generalize on the basis of yourself; that is, to presume that your partner is exactly like you in terms of hurts, habits, preferences, hopes, and expectations. Indeed, we all fall in love with, and are mesmerized by, the magic of another human being precisely because that person is different from us. But all too often once we're in a relationship, we behave as if our mate is just an extension of ourselves.

This is visible in the matrimonial "we." "We don't like big cities." "We don't like swordfish." "We always …" "We never …" And it's invisible, but often present, in our private assumptions: "Because I like vacations in the mountains, so should you;" "Because I get up at the crack of dawn, so should you;" "Because I want kids, you will too;" "Because I express love in words, you will too." Countless fights come out of the seemingly harmless presumptions that because I do, so will (or should) you.

Expecting another person to be a clone of yourself is an emotional hangover from infancy when, indeed, you were the center of the universe. When we were babies, the world *did* revolve around us—if we woke up screaming at 5:00 a.m., then everybody else woke up too. But in adulthood, when you treat your sweetheart as if he or she is just like you, you reduce that person to a kind of nonentity. You say, in effect, it's only my consciousness, my way of doing things, my preferences that matter here—what you feel or think is irrelevant.

The antidote to this spirit-squashing is to learn to do one very simple thing: inquire. Explore. Ask. Let curiosity help you discover what your mate wants and needs from you. The more you know precisely what he or she is, the less you'll make this person-erasing mistake.

In the long run, remembering that the person you love is not you is a way of exposing yourself to the joy of knowing another soul in the truth and beauty of who he or she actually is. And it's celebrating the difference that's really what love is all about.

Don't Make Assumptions

Assumptions—saying something that presumes you know what another person is thinking, feeling, or doing—always hurt the person about whom they're made and create a barrier to intimacy. Remarks like "You don't care about me as much as I care about you," "You don't have to worry about money," "You don't have much to do today," all have the effect of closing down the other person and limiting reality to our interpretation of it. Basically we are saying, "I know who you are and what's going on with you and I don't need your version of the story."

Assumptions usually feel like a violation of spirit to the person who is theoretically being perceived. They are a reduction of the true complexity of reality and a negation of the other person's essence, taking away his or her uniqueness and freedom of expression. Assumptions close off possibilities by making people withdraw and hide out even more. Eliminating them opens the flow of real conversation in which lovers can show their real selves, and discover the beautiful particulars of one another.

Honor Your Relationship in Public

Your relationship, just like you, has a self-image. You and your beloved came together to express, among other things, the fact that the union of two people is a worthy and beautiful thing. Holding your relationship and the other person in high regard means you will also treat it in public as the treasure you know it to be.

Honoring your relationship in public means that you will not provocatively (or in any other way) flirt with somebody else, nor will you thoughtlessly compare your honey to others, make fun of the person you love, nor rudely fight in the presence of others.

Don't turn your darling into a sourpuss at the party (or a disinterested lover when you get home) by staring too long at the statuesque blonde. Don't make your beloved feel inadequate by leaning too close or talking too long to the rock star who just showed up at the benefit dinner. And don't make yourself look like you picked the wrong guy by putting your sweetheart down at the neighborhood Fourth of July barbeque.

Of course she has faults. Of course he isn't perfect. But nobody else needs to know it. Don't announce it to the world—it's none of their business. And don't compare your sweetheart's anything—looks, manners, attributes, foibles, or bank account—to anybody you met at the party. It doesn't feel good to be compared.

Love needs to be nurtured, not threatened and abused. Honoring your relationship in public means that you care enough to keep your honey comfortable, care enough to have the outside world stand in honor—or in awe—of the person you chose and the relationship you created.

Find Your Joy and Share It

In the past, many women were martyrs to their partners and families: ("I ironed sixteen shirts and he didn't even thank me," "The kids walked all over my clean kitchen floor and didn't even notice") and now we're slaves to the double masters of work and family: "I worked all day and I still had to make the dinner;" "My boss bawls me out for being late to work and my husband's mad because we didn't make love this morning."

It is hard to find joy in days as crammed as most of our days seem to be. But for the joy of yourself and the bliss of your relationship, ask yourself, would I rather be a martyr or the creator of an inspired life? What little—or big—action can you take today on your own behalf so that when you engage with your partner you will be full of light and delight? A yoga class? A morning walk? Meditating? Making yourself some healthy food? Give yourself joy, nurturing, and time. The joy you have yourself is a gift you give to your relationship.

Forgive One Another

To forgive is to see the person who has offended you in an entirely different way, through the eyes of charity and love. This is a difficult, but life-transforming task, for forgiveness breathes new life into a relationship and changes the chemistry between you from stale to sweet.

In a real sense, forgiveness begins with yourself, with the understanding that despite your best intentions, you too will fail, will find yourself doing the terrible things you thought only your enemies were capable of doing. To see yourself with compassion in spite of your failures is the beginning of forgiveness for others. For we can never take back into our hearts the person who has wounded us unless we can first be kind to ourselves about our own offenses.

Forgiveness requires emotional maturity and a willingness to move yourself into the future. To forgive is to start over, in a different place, to behave from the depths of your heart as if the bad thing never happened. In this sense forgiveness is a creative act; it invites you to create a new and more conscious relationship.

Kindle the Romance

Romance is the champagne and frosted glasses of love, the magic that gives love a tango to dance to, a fragrance to remember, and a fantasy-come-true to hold in your heart. Romance is the antidote to ordinariness, the inspiration for passion; whenever you fold it into your relationship, you instantly elevate it to a more delicious state of being. Romanced, you feel beautiful or handsome; life becomes ripe with hope; the moon, stars, and planets bathe you in a cascade of beneficent light; and you believe everything is possible—your sweetest, wildest, and most cherished dreams will certainly come true.

At least that's certainly how we feel in the rosy blush of new romance. But the feeling of romance doesn't just stick around all by itself. As time goes on, it takes effort, ingenuity, intuition, and sometimes even a willingness to feel foolish, to keep the moonlight magical. That's because somewhere along the line, without quite paying attention, we stop doing the things that kindled romance in the first place: we forget to bring the roses, to whisper the sweet nothings, we leave the lights on (or off), we trade in the black lingerie for flannel pajamas. In short, we start treating one another as roommates instead of passionate lovers.

You can all still have romance in your life, no matter how long you and your sweetheart have been together. All it takes is a conscious remembering to chill the glasses, remember the roses, light the candles, and once in a while play the song you listened to when you first fell in love. Passion breeds intimacy, romance brings feelings of connection. So c'mon—dress the bed in red sheets, pack a picnic, then drive up the hill to watch the sunset and kiss (and kiss and kiss) in the car.

Do the Unexpected

Sarah surprised her husband, Matt, by appearing at his office on his birthday in black net stockings, top hot and tails, carrying a cake and singing "Happy Birthday."

Jim told Abby he had to pick up some film for his new camera and would she come along for the ride? Then he drove to the park, unloaded a picnic basket from the trunk of the car, revealed a gorgeous bouquet of red roses and, under the spreading elms, asked her to marry him.

Everybody (well almost everybody) likes a surprise, the uninvited appearance of the totally unexpected, the unusual, the hidden treasure, the silver lining. The unanticipated event leaves us happily off kilter, so spice up your life by doing something completely different. Throw gardenia petals on the bed, put a love note in the freezer, read each other a bedtime story, bury tickets to the circus under the pillow, take your honey to a fortune teller, leave a secret erotic message on his answering machine, call her at work just to tell her you love her, serve a candlelight dinner in bed. Pretend you're asleep and then wake your spouse up to make love.

Do the unexpected—whatever it is and as often as you can—and watch as love turns from dishwasher dull to the sparkle of champagne.

Be Creative

When it comes to romance, be creative, even if at first you feel shy or embarrassed. Remember, you weren't embarrassed by all the love notes and love songs when you were first falling in love. The art of romance takes imagination. The more you stretch the limits, the more inventive you'll become, especially if your initial efforts engender a positive response.Whatever your particular romantic preferences may be, be sure to indulge them as much as you can, and maybe they'll give you some new ideas too. Don't let opportunities slip through the cracks. Like the love it will embellish, romance is a very special art form whose reward is the joy of passion. So use your imagination—and your discipline.

Play, Play, Play

When we play we feel the carefree joyfulness of our spirits. We're delivered from the bonds of obligation and responsibility to a sense of delight about ourselves. Playing allows you to rekindle the sense of the child in yourself, to go back to a time when life was new and full of possibility. Because inside we are all still young, we need to play as much as we can.

Playing alone or with others—a round of golf, an aerobics class, a soccer game, a tennis match—isn't just frivolous nonsense. Play creates balance. It's the safety net under the tightrope of modern life; it keeps us sane and functioning.

Playing alone is good. Playing together is better. Playing with the person you love is the premier form of play. Playing combines both the intrinsic joys of play with the opportunity to have a totally carefree experience (and sometimes mind-altering view) of the person you love. Seeing and being with him at his most spontaneous, at her most innocent and unguarded, can only deepen your appreciation of him, your sense of her specialness. For when we do what we love, you are most precisely yourself. Besides, shared foolishness deepens bonds, and gives you happy carefree things to remember.

"Remember when we held the croquet tournament over Labor Day and you won?" "Remember when we went to the MacIntoshes' Halloween party and I was a ballerina and you were a cat?" "Remember the summer we played badminton on the back lawn every single night after supper?"

Sweet memories are strong glue in any relationship. So play often; play hard; play for fun, and play for keeps.

Kiss Each Other Hello and Goodbye

Remember how, when you were falling in love, you couldn't wait to see each other, couldn't wait to hold his hand, to kiss her lips? How leaving each other was pure torture, a heartbreak to be postponed as long as possible? Just because the fires of new romance have become the steady embers of real love doesn't mean that you don't still need the blessing of coming together and departing from each other with a loving ritual.

When you come back together with a loving welcome, you acknowledge that you are re-entering the presence and spirit of the person you love, and that you are doing so happily. By departing with a special farewell, you put a loving seal on each other, showing that you don't take one another for granted.

If you are going away on a business trip, don't just pack up your bags and disappear. Take your husband into your arms and tell him that you'll miss him. Or, when you walk in the door, put down your briefcase, and stop to kiss your wife. Don't just waltz in with an "I'm home" and head for the den and the mail. And if you're the one who gets home first, don't just lie on the couch glued to the TV, without so much as a word of greeting. Sit up, get up, make contact, and kiss. Look into each other's eyes.

And above all, don't open the exchange of your reuniting with a "What took you so long?" "Where the hell have you been?" or "Why isn't dinner ready?" Before you get on with the facts and demands of real life, *stop* and acknowledge the person with whom you have chosen to share your life.

If all this hugging and kissing seems silly, remind yourself that we never really know, do we, that we will see one another again. So even the smallest reunion is a tiny miracle.

Do it Again and Again and Again

There's a gypsy I know who will read your palm, and answer any two questions for ten dollars. If there's anything amiss in your life, a wish that's hard to make true, she always asks for a hundred dollars so she can burn ten candles for ten days and light your wish into reality.

I've always wondered whether she really burns the candles or if it's just a hype for more money; but either way, she has a point: wishes don't come true by wishing them just once. They become actualized through effort and attention and just as the gypsy lights the candles to ensure results, it's holding the flame of desire in our hearts and minds, in our emotions and actions, that brings our most heart-felt wishes into being.

Behavior is difficult to change. It takes practice and repetition. This is no less true about the behaviors of love. Learning to think differently about the person you love and incorporating new emotional behaviors is a process that takes time. You won't learn the actions of love in a minute, nor will they become your possessions simply by reading this book. You will have to remember them and act them out over and over again in order to get permanent results.

The behaviors of love affect us like nourishment: when we're hungry, we eat and are satisfied. But this doesn't mean that we won't be hungry again, that we won't need again to be filled. Just because you remembered once to kindle the romance or to acknowledge the hardships your circumstances created, doesn't mean that you've done it for all time. We need the benedictions and courtesies of love to be repeated over and over again. None of us has been so blessed and indulged that we don't need all the good things we can possibly get.

Like a wish or a work of art, the beauty of a relationship is sculpted over time. The love you desire will become yours only through a constancy of effort. So do all these things over and over again, and your relationship will surely flourish, far beyond your imagining.

4

The Art and Practice
of Loving Communication

Practice Good Communication

F ar and away, the thing people complain most about in their relationships is "lack of communication." What they're really saying is that they don't feel truly known in ways that make them feel close and loved. This is because most people don't believe they can be known. In our secret heart of hearts we all fear that we are alone in the universe and that no one will really understand us. This is why we all long for meaningful communication.

Contrary to our expectations, however, communication isn't just talking, getting your own point across or being sure you've been heard. Far more than we imagine, communication is also receptive. It's listening, taking in, absorbing, and allowing yourself to be changed by what has been said to you. Without listening, talking can be a one-sided enterprise, leaving the arc of communication incomplete. But when both talking and listening occur, a conversation gains antiphony and both partners have the sense that they now occupy a common ground.

The place of deep connection doesn't just happen in a relationship. It is arrived at through the steady practice of the art of communication on the intellectual, sexual, and emotional planes.

Satisfying communication takes courage. It requires reaching beyond the trivial for the deeper truth of who you are and what you feel, and the willingness to take the risk of showing yourself to another person. True communication is also receptive. It indicates that you love enough to be affected—moved, challenged, transformed—by what you have heard.

Because communication has the capacity to bond us at the deepest, most unspoken levels, true communication is an interpersonal miracle. It allows us to get inside each other's skins, to know and be known by another human being. It is the means by which we throw open the windows of our own souls and let the light of another's soul shine in. If you seek more meaning in your relationship, practice, risk, and learn the art of true communication.

Learn the Language of Intimacy

If you think of yourself as protected by many layers of emotional cotton batting, intimacy represents the gradual unwrapping of these layers until you stand in another's presence with the secrets of your heart unveiled. Intimacy is achieved through communication that springs from our depths and reaches to our depths. The more we partake of such communication, the greater our sense that we are not alone; in fact, the greater our sense that at the core we're all deeply connected.

The communication of intimacy is an art form all its own. It has its own style. Unlike the conversations of business, which focus on facts and figures, or the language of recreation, which often takes the form of planning—what movie to go to, where to get the best pastries—the communication of intimacy springs from emotion and

uses language which is, by definition, personal. It uses the word I—
I need, *I* feel, *I'm* having a difficult day; *I* love you so deeply—and it
focuses on feelings.

Indeed, the communications that create the deepest sense of intimacy are the clear, strong, beautiful words through which we bring out the feelings we have deep inside. When you express your feelings (as opposed to opinions or ideas), you create intimacy because you're showing your real self.

You'll find the exact words for your feelings when you look inside and ask: What am I feeling? What do I need to say right now? After you've seen what you feel, try to simply and directly put your feelings into words.

Remember that whatever you feel—your secret hopes, your feelings of shame or inadequacy, your fears, your hurt—deserves to be expressed. When you express these feelings out loud, you open a window to the sensitive inner corridors of your being and invite your beloved to shine a light in. You create intimacy.

Tie Up Your Emotional Loose Ends

E motional loose ends are those little nagging things that stand between you and your mate: unexpressed resentments, unbandaged hurts, unresolved conflicts, unmentioned little embarrassments, requests that are hiding in the background. Unsaid, they spoil your emotional bond, clouding the clarity you'd like to have with one another.

When you tie up emotional loose ends, instead of letting your conflicts and difficulties fester in the slough of non-expression, you bring them to a conclusion and make peace with one another before going on. Doing this implies that you both desire and believe you can bring your union to a place of emotional calm, in which you can once again take the risks that can deepen your relationship.

A relationship needs a consistent, ground level of harmony, a safe place from which the people in it can take the chances that enhance their own growth and nurture the bonds that connect them. Tying up your emotional loose ends is a way of keeping this sanctuary clear.

We all have a tendency to let things go, to hope that whatever's amiss will just work itself out or disappear. Some things do become conveniently irrelevant in time, but the truth is that not resolving emotional issues also takes an incredible amount of energy.

For example, Yvonne was still mad at Cliff about a fight they'd had on Friday. When they went out on Saturday night, instead of being able to relax and enjoy herself, she was cranky and unsettled. Something he'd said in passing—"It's insane how much you talk on the phone with your friend Laura"—had particularly hurt her. Yvonne relied on the funny and supportive chats with Laura, and it was scary to think that Cliff could have such a negative reaction. But instead of telling him about it, she "hoped he didn't really mean it," or that "he'd get over it." She even thought about making a snide remark about Cliff's best friend, Ned, the next time the two of them went golfing. But none of these efforts to shove things under the rug had worked. Yvonne was still upset, and not talking about it only had the effect of spoiling their Saturday night.

This is a perfect example of how emotional loose ends can turn into romantic nooses. So instead of building a gallows for your love, take time and care to resolve your emotional business, no matter how trite or inconsequential it may seem. Love blossoms under blue skies, and tying up your emotional loose ends shoos all the storm clouds away.

Look for the Message Under the Words

At a party recently, a dear friend of mine arrived extremely late. When I went over to give her a hug a few minutes later, I could feel that she didn't really receive it. Instead of responding, she started talking in an offhanded way about being late. She'd had to visit her brother, who was in the hospital; there was a traffic jam; it was raining. "Where are the hors d'oeurves?" she finally asked. "I'm starving." About then, I put my hand on her arm, looked her straight in the eye and said, "Sarah, you don't have to be so brave." Leaning her head on my shoulder, she said, "I'm so scared he's not going to make it," and then she started bawling like a child.

What we say is often not what we mean. Our true feelings are frequently hidden in the intricate secret spaces between the words we utter. Most of us don't have the language to put the full extent of our feelings into words, and lots of times we're not even sure what we're feeling. For most of us, expressing our feelings precisely is extremely difficult. This is especially true when what we're feeling is sorrow, vulnerability, or shame. In the presence of such emotions, our words are often pitifully inaccurate, and what we reveal with our eyes and bodies is a much truer representation of our real message.

When love listens, it listens with an ear and a heart to the unspoken. So when you listen to others, attend also to what they aren't saying in words. Reach for the hidden meanings, the meanings that are being expressed through the twitching finger, the heaving chest, the furrowed brow, the tear-clouded eye. Listen with your heart and your eyes, and respond to the message under the words.

In Conflict, Seek the Common Ground

When conflict arises, we need to look for the common ground. In the midst of the fray, when you seek the kernel of truth that can bridge you back to understanding, you can find your way once again to union.

We all have a dark side; we've all hurt one another more than we'd like to admit. But even our misdeeds are worth an attempt at understanding, because the truth is that even dastardly acts are born of pain. That doesn't excuse them, of course, but it's important to remember that even the hurtful things that we do spring from the woundedness within us. When I can comprehend your suffering (and, therefore, the crooked behavior you perpetrated on me) and you can comprehend my pain (and therefore my wrongdoing to you), we can stand face-to-face in compassion, unravel the missteps we've made, and together start over from a different place.

So if in your heart of hearts, you seek union, pleasure, companionship, support, and nourishment from the person you love, don't make an adversary out of him or her. Even in the hairiest fray, try curiosity and kindness—"Why were you late?" "Why were you so short with me?"—and you may find out something surprising ("I got back a frightening mammogram today." "The guy right next to me in the gym keeled over dead."), something which, instead of turning your beloved into the enemy, will fill your heart with compassion.

Be Sensitive About Timing

Relationships themselves and every event, behavior, and action within them have their own unique and perfect timing. Just as the ideal mate often shows up only when you've completely given up ever falling in love, so it is that within a relationship there are perfect moments for everything, a choreography of timing that can either support or detract from the grace of your relationship.

Timing is a sensitive reflection of myriad things about us: our histories ("I can't stand to do the dishes right after dinner because my mother was so compulsive she'd start washing the dishes before we even finished our dessert"), our metabolisms ("I'm just not a morning person"), our methods of apprehending reality ("I'll never get it if you talk about it for an hour; tell me what you need, let me go for a walk, and I'll be able to give you an answer when I get back"), our emotional sensitivities ("I just can't handle more than one complaint at a time; my father used to sit me down and read a list of all my mistakes for the week"), and our just plain personal quirks ("I don't know why—I just wake up at 4:00 a.m.").

Sensitivity about timing adds grace to any union. If, together, you don't cultivate this sensitivity, you'll be continually jamming up against the differences in your time frames, saying the emotionally loaded thing at an inauspicious moment, or generally feeling abused in the realm of time. Conversely, when you learn to choose the perfect moment—to say the heart-touching words, to present the sapphire ring—you'll turn your relationship into a beautifully choreographed performance of the exquisite dance of your love.

Say the Love Words

*E*verybody wants to hear how much, and precisely why, he or she is loved. Even when you've been chosen, even after you've tied the knot, you'll still need the verbal reassurance that you are loved.

We need to be endeared, to feel that we are special, delightful, precious, irreplaceable to the one we love. We want to be singled out, to be told we are loved above all by the person who has chosen us.

We often think that having a feeling about someone is as good as saying it, but it isn't. Make no mistake—words mean a lot to all of us. We all walk around with a huge collection of insecurities, and none of us is so sure, so cut and dried in our conviction about our own self-worth that we don't need the inspiration of being told every which way, over and over again, exactly why, how, and how much we are loved.

We need to be told, and the words have to be heartfelt. There's just no comparison between the abstract "Of course I love you" and the direct "I love you," no contest between silence and "You're the light of my life; I want to be with you forever."

Even though some people may think it is corny, in the delicate layers of even the coolest of cucumber hearts is a lover who yearns to be adored. There's a hidden romantic in each of us, the person who fell in love, who was tantalized by music and moonlight, who waited breathlessly to hear the words that heralded new love: "I adore you. I can't live without you." And once isn't—and never will be—enough. For even if we could we don't want to have to keep the faith about love. We want our hearts to be filled by hearing the love words over and over again.

Love words are a tonic for love, an elixir for passion, a medicinal balm for fading romance. Life is infested with ordinariness, and there isn't any reason why love should be too. Words are the wings of romance, the way in which, more than any other, we elevate ourselves above the ordinary and pedestrian. Nothing can sustain the high pitch of romance better than beautiful love words, generously and end-lessly spoken. Find the words that express your love and speak them.

Fight Well, Fight Fair

No relationship is without conflict—and a relationship is only as good as the conflict it can contain. All too often, couples in tran-quil relationships are scared of testing the resilience of their rela-tionship by airing their real differences, or they have so suppressed their individuality that their differences seem invisible.

Many of us are scared of conflict simply because we don't know how to fight. We're afraid our anger will run away with us, that we'll lose control and become vicious or even physically destructive. We're also afraid of the other person's anger—will he or she yell, throw things, slam the door, or walk out. The good news is that it's possi-ble to express anger in a constructive way, and the sign of a good fight is that it makes you both feel you have discovered something, that you know each other better. Even if you fight again and again about the same issues (and most of us do), a good fight gives you hope about the future because after it, you know you've gained insight about something that previously baffled or frustrated you.

Here's some help:

- Try to see what you're angry about. This is usually something very specific: "That you didn't call," not "Because life is miserable."

- State your feeling and why you feel that way: "I'm angry that you didn't call because it makes me feel unloved."

- Say what you need in recompense: "I need you to apologize."

- After your mate has given the apology, ask yourself and him or her if you feel totally resolved.

- Kiss and make up.

For example, "I'm angry at you for yelling at me about burning the toast. You embarrassed me in front of Kay. It made me feel belittled to have her hear you talk to me like that. I need you to apologize."

"I'm sorry, honey. I was in a rush this morning and anxious about that big meeting. I was out of line. I don't want to make you feel that way. Please forgive me."

This, of course, would win the Academy Award for Most Civilized Fight, and with your high feelings and sense of frustration over the number of times the hateful thing has happened, to say nothing of your just plain humanness, you probably won't always be able to muster quite so much graciousness. In any case, try to remember:

- A good fight isn't a free-for-all. Don't say everything you feel like saying even though you may have a legitimate gripe. Remember that words can wound, and after the fight you don't want a battered mate.

- Be specific with your complaints. Don't throw in all your grievances since time began.

- Let the other person's words sink in before you take up your cudgel. Remember, you're having this fight to learn something, to arrive at some new insight as well as an immediate resolution.

- Go easy on yourself and your honey when you don't do it perfectly.

For Men: Stop Communicating in Code

Verbal communication represents the broadest common denominator in human interactions. Both men and women use language to conduct their business, whether it be emotional business or the larger, more complex transactions of running the world. For the most part, we all know the meaning of a given word, and because of their agreed-upon meanings, words are generally much easier to interpret than actions. In a sense, words are the universal communication code. Men, though, have a lot of non-verbal ways of communicating. Sex, of course, is one. So is bringing flowers. So is fixing the washing machine. So is slamming the door and walking around the block before continuing the conversation. This is what I call communicating in code.

While communicating in code does carry emotional meanings that women should learn to divine, it's also true that a lot of the time both partners need to use words, the preferred communication medium of women. Communication by code can never cover the range nor equal the power, the intricacy, and beauty that can be created through the use of language. If men want to have truly satisfying relationships with women, difficult though it is, they'll have to start venturing out from the pure-male position of communicating in code and start practicing the art of direct verbal expression that women already know is rewarding.

C'mon, guys; start talking.

Learn to Say What You Feel

Feelings reside in us like a river and pass through our consciousness in an ever-moving flow. Revealing your emotional tides to the person you love is a way for you to continue to endear yourself to and amaze your partner. We often think that intimacy is created merely by falling in love or by what we do, plan, buy, or pursue together. But it is actually the getting to know another person through the intricate texture of his or her emotions that makes us feel truly connected. In fact an intimate relationship at its core is a process of trading feelings to a high degree.

Indeed it is this revelation of feelings that continues to deepen our level of intimacy with one another. For it is in our feelings, our capacity to be delighted and disappointed, to grieve, to be afraid, to want, to feel the loss of, that we dip into the common human stream and connect with one another at the deepest level. This is why, when you say what you feel, your partner discovers him or herself through you.

If it's difficult for you to express your emotions, what you need to know is that it will be worth it to step into these curiously unfamiliar waters and discover the treasures at your depths. Not only will your partner be pleased to connect with you in this way, but the experience of discovering and identifying your feelings will give you a greater sense of richness about your own inner life. Therefore, let the person you love enter the underground stream of your feelings so he can cherish you, so she can love you even more, by starting to say, exactly and always, whatever is in your heart and mind.

Start Asking for What You Need

Asking for what you need is just that: stating that there is something amiss about which you need some care or response. "Would you please close the window? I'm freezing." "I need you to hold me; I'm scared." "Will you give me a back rub? My shoulder hurts." Asking for what you need is such a simple yet difficult thing that most of us rarely, if ever, do it. In fact, it is so hard (or easy) that most of us would rather try almost anything else than to ask quite simply and directly for precisely what we need. We would rather presume that our sweetheart will know without our telling, or hope that in time our spouse will, by osmosis, figure it out. Often we'd just as soon give up on getting the thing we need rather than actually having to ask for it.

We don't like to ask because we think of asking as revealing neediness—which is precisely what it is. Asking means we are in a vulnerable state and that we are hoping the other person will care enough to minister to us in our pitiful, imperfect, and inadequate condition.

Asking for what you need reveals the true fragileness of your humanity, and invites the person who loves you to expand the range of his or her own. Responding to a stated request not only gives the needy person the relief of having his need fulfilled; it also gives the giver a sense of being able to be effective, to offer a gift of value. On these occasions, you are both enjoined to expand the range of your love and your humanity. It might feel strange to you, but start asking for what you need—you just might get it.

Stop Being an Emotional Chicken

A lot us are emotional chickens, afraid to communicate what we are really feeling. Emotional chickens are worried that what they disclose will be ignored, made fun of, or ridiculed, so rather than taking the risk of spitting it out—whatever it is—they just keep quiet. Often they even defend their shut-down stance, saying that talking about feelings never does any good anyway.

Being an emotional chicken has old, sad origins. It begins when we aren't listened to as children, when we were told that the things we said were unimportant or when we sensed that no one could feel with us our private anguish. Feeling this way made us scared. And fear taught us to keep our thoughts and feelings to ourselves.

If you're an emotional chicken, it isn't only the big secrets that you're afraid to tell. Many of us are uncomfortable saying anything that might be construed as even slightly confrontational. "I don't want to go to the Taj Mahal Café, I want to go to the Bean Sprout Club for dinner." "I'm angry at you for not making love to me last night." But of course it's precisely the things you are afraid of telling your sweetheart that will show him or her who you really are.

Here's how to stop being an emotional chicken: Whenever you're having the slightly unsettled feeling that comes from not saying what's on your mind, try asking yourself: What is it that I'm not saying? Usually the words are right in your mind like in one of those little cartoon balloons. Then ask yourself: Why am I not saying it right *now*? Maybe there's a good reason—he just got fired from his job, the kids are both crying, you have to walk out the door in five minutes for a business meeting, your mother-in-law is on the phone. In such cases, you probably should hold your comments for later. But if there isn't a good, practical reason for not speaking *now*, just open your mouth and spit out the words that are dying to escape. You'll feel better, and you'll be making the first step toward being emotionally brave. So start risking now.

Keep Your Criticisms Private

We all do things that are less than perfect—some of us talk too fast or interrupt constantly; others are perpetually late, sloppy about housekeeping or perfectionistic in our work habits. The things we do wrong are enough of an embarrassment to us that we certainly don't need to be reminded about them in public.

Registering such seemingly innocent or small time complaints as "You never remember to take out the garbage," or "You always spill on your new clothes; you're such a mess" even jokingly in the presence of friends, dinner guests, the plumber, your aunt, or a mother-in-law, is degrading to another's person's essence. It has the effect of making him or her feel small, worthless, and punished in the presence of people among whom he or she would like to feel whole, effective, and worthy.

It doesn't do much to solidify your relationship either. How much will you feel like helping your wife take the car to the garage if, when you show up at her office, she says in front of her boss that she can't believe how long it took you to get here?

Reprimands always have painful reference to childhood. They harken back to a haunting sense of inadequacy, and the feelings of powerlessness that were the hallmarks of being small and at the mercy of our parents. For this reason, it is doubly painful to be reminded of our flaws, shortcomings, and failures in front of anyone except our intimate dear ones, whom we may legitimately hope will try to understand and forgive.

It's true that we all have creepy little inadequacies that bear remarking on, and when they're noted in private, we can be inspired to change. Indeed criticism, like encouragement, can shape the direction of our path and therefore serves a wonderfully creative function.

But when criticism is leveled in public, it diminishes our dignity and, far from correcting whatever needs to be improved, makes us skittish and afraid. Rather than being an invitation to change, reprimanding is a spirit-breaking act. Preserve your love by graciously keeping silent about the things you'd like to correct until you're in the privacy of one another's arms.

Hold Your Tongue

After years of his wife Jana's steadfast labor and infinite patience helping him do research and typing his doctoral dissertation, John carelessly said to her in a fight, "Who needs you anyway? You've never done a thing for me." Jana was crushed. She told me afterwards she felt as if a bomb had gone off inside her. She went to the bedroom, took out a suitcase, packed some clothes, and moved into a motel. It took months of negotiations and therapy before she and John could reconcile.

The moral of the story? Be careful what you say. Being upset is no excuse to get carried away in a fight and assassinate your loved one's character. Sticks and stones may break your bones, but words always have the potential of creating deep and sometimes even irreversible hurts. Comments about a person's intelligence, body, value, or ability to love (to say nothing of comparisons with past lovers, sweethearts, or spouses) can, in fact, shake your mate to the core. We don't like to think that something said in anger could have a lasting effect, but it can. Nasty remarks can be so devastating as to permanently mar the self-esteem of the other person or irrevocably damage the goodwill of your relationship.

So avoid the gratuitous mean-spirited remark. "Well, you can just go get a divorce then." "You never loved me anyway." "You've never understood me." "You're too fat." "I'm going back to John. At least he knew how to make love."

Whether we know it or not, we all have a kind of cruel sixth sense about the words that can really devastate our partners. We all know the sensitive, vulnerable place, the spiritual Achilles heel in which he or she can be mortally bruised. That's why we need to hold our tongues. Think twice or a dozen times, count to ten or ten hundred, before you say the thing that could devastate your partner.

Apologize, Apologize, Apologize

It's really very simple, but so very hard to do. When you make a mistake, apologize: "I'm sorry. You're right. I did forget to pick up the dry cleaning. Please forgive me." "I'm sorry I yelled. I know I scared you." "I'm sorry I wasn't listening. I do want to hear what you're saying."

Acknowledging both your flaws as a person and also your specific boo-boos—the small and big mistakes, the rotten little things you do or forget to do—is the great janitorial broom of a good relationship. It clears the debris from the path to your loved one's heart, a path that can all too easily get cluttered with nagging little resentments. Apologizing is a way of keeping current with your relationship, of making sure that the two of you aren't loving through a window so fogged by old complaints that it's impossible to see or be seen clearly by one another.

Apology consists of three essential parts: stating your crimes by name, saying you're sorry, and asking to be forgiven. It differs radically from defensiveness. When we are defensive, we become lawyers for our own case; "I did it because . . . ," "I didn't mean to do it," "He or she made me do it," "It's all in your mind," "It was no big deal."

All these defensive postures have the effect of muddying the emotional waters. They obscure our true shortcomings, flaws, and mistakes, and require that we be loved at a shallow level—the level of self-deception—and not at the depth of our emotional integrity. When we own up to our mistakes, we ask that we be loved in the full measure of our humanness, imperfect though we may be. And when we reveal this humanness, we magically and instantly expand the quality of our relationships.

Talk About Your Fears

In an intimate relationship, there aren't any extra points for being brave. In fact, bravery is fakery, the antithesis of intimacy. To have a truly meaningful relationship, you need to be willing to talk about what you're afraid of.

For a number of reasons, we're all ashamed of being afraid. Men especially are taught that fears are for sissies and that, when we finally "get it together," we will have transcended our fears.

The truth is that our fears arise from some very tender places in ourselves, areas where we've been hurt, where we haven't quite grown up, where we're not yet emotionally resilient enough to feel strong in the face of the scary things that life is doling out to us. Our fears are as various as the petty fear of spiders or the fear of our own mortality. But no matter how inconsequential or overwhelming your fears may be, they're reports from the fragile interior of your psyche. In revealing them, you'll give your partner access to the places where you need to be nurtured; where, because of your vulnerabilities, you are most in need of love.

Unveiling your fears is an act of openness that counts on a loving response. It compliments your lover because it says, "I know you love me enough to allow me to show you my weakness and I trust you to be careful with me." So take the risk of revealing your fears, and your revelations will be twice blessed. They will bless you as you are relieved of your fears, and your lover will be blessed with the chance to console you.

Tell Your Story

*E*specially if you've been in a relationship for a long time, you may think you know your partner. We all do, of course, know a whole array of things about one another when we're in a relationship, but it's really only when we tell our stories—the touching vignettes that embody our struggles, sweet moments, disappointments, or wild hopes and dreams—that our most vulnerable selves are revealed. Indeed, if we don't tell each other our stories, we're all one-dimensional, blank screens on which we project our assumptions about one another.

Everybody has a story, and because we all do, when we hear each other's stories, we feel suddenly connected. Story is the great river that runs through the human landscape, and our individual stories are the little creeks that flow through us all to join the river at its source. When you tell your story, you open yourself to the level of fragility which, as human beings, we all share. For, no matter how different our stories, at the bottom of each of them is the well of pain from which we have all dipped a draught.

Tell your darling your story—the most painful event of your childhood, the most exciting moment, the greatest regret of your adult life—and you will discover, in depth, a self you never knew. That's because, between the sentences of your stories, the gist of things slips out, not merely the facts, but the feelings that have shaped you, the point, in anyone's journey, from which there was no return. Your stories are your true self, spelled out and spoken, brought forth in time and in your own language, a gift of deep revelation you can give to the person you love.

Share Your Dreams

*Y*our dreams, whether the ones you have at night or the hopes and aspirations you have for your life, represent some of the most profound, protected, and precious parts of yourself. Because they're so private, the minute you share them you create intimacy.

Images from your sleep are a map of your uncensored self. They are messages to and about you from the deepest reaches of your unconscious. In the enigmatic language of your own private symbols, they reveal the secrets you keep even from yourself.

Telling your sweetheart your dreams is an act of sharing, for in opening the door to your unconscious in this way, you are allowing the person you love to meet you in a special and unguarded place, the place of magic, often beyond common sense or even words. Whether or not your dreams make sense to you or your partner (and you don't have to be Sigmund Freud to receive at least a few of their meanings), being given a view of your beloved through this mysterious looking glass is to be taken into his or her spiritual privacy.

The same is true of the dreams that are your aspirations. For in revealing your hopes and longings you become at once most exalted and most vulnerable. In speaking of what you desire you also reveal how you can be disappointed. The fact that you always wanted to be a ballerina (and can't even walk across the living room without banging into the coffee table) is something you don't want everyone to know, but telling that to the person you love is a way of revealing a sensitive part of yourself.

None of us can live out all our dreams—life isn't long enough. And we all have more talents than time to explore them in. Although on some level we realize that this is true, there's also a sense of loss attached to letting go of even our most ridiculous dreams. When you share your unfulfilled dreams, you're asking your sweetheart to love you not only for who you are, but also for who you would like to have been.

Revealing your dreams is also an act of trust. It means you believe that the person who loves you can see you in your secret essence without being horrified or ashamed. So take the risk of sharing your innermost secrets, and know that should your aspirations turn to ashes, the person you love will still be there to comfort you.

Have the Courage to Say No

We are defined in life and in love not only by what we have the fortitude to undertake but also by what we have the courage to resist. In the long-ago movie, Days of Wine and Roses, a man and woman descended into a wildly gyrating spiral of alcoholism, all the while egging each other on. Finally, the man said "No" to himself, and, eventually, to his wife.

Life doesn't always ask us for such intense denunciations, nor is the path to our no's always so excruciatingly painful. But we all have things that we have to say no to—for ourselves and in our relationships—or else move in a direction that isn't for our highest good.

Sometimes these no's are small and simple, an unadorned statement of preference that's a quiet affirmation of your right to be yourself: "No, I don't want to go to the late show; I'll be too tired for work in the morning." "No, I don't want dessert." "No, I don't want to go to the party." Sometimes they ask for more strength, require that you actually take a stand: "No, I don't want to buy a . . .; we're already too much in debt." Sometimes they involve issues of life and death: "No, I won't give up my AA meeting just because you'd like me at home on Tuesday night."

Having the courage to say no means that you trust yourself and your relationship. It means you believe that your bond has the strength and resilience to absorb your no, as well as the power, as a consequence, to grow—in well-being, in moral fortitude. In saying no, you exercise the faith that the two of you, together, can live by the values represented by your no, recognizing that these values will take you to a level higher than the one embodied by the things that you are choosing to resist.

A no is a choice for the good, the true, and the beautiful, and, in relationships, for the power, the beauty, and the possibilities of the relationship itself. Have the courage to say no!

Seek the Deliverance Point

The deliverance point is that exquisite moment in any personal encounter or life experience in which we arrive at a state of resolution about what has troubled, violated, or detained us; and we stand free to move to the next level of our unfolding.

Getting to the deliverance point isn't easy. We want to be magically lifted up out of the conflict, whatever it is: the horrible, repetitive, seemingly insoluble argument; the hateful job; the gnawing feeling of insecurity; a particular chronic irritation (his tardiness, her raucous laughter); the vague feeling of alienation that, in general, we are quietly subjected to by living in such a fast-changing world. We want to reach the deliverance point, but often don't want to pay the price, which is going through instead of around whatever the problem is.

To arrive at the place of the "Aha! I've made it out of the pit of hell," we need to be willing to crawl on emotional all-fours to get to the destination. This means, in a relationship, being willing to have the fight (whether you're scared of your anger or not); to initiate the discussion (whether or not you feel foolish); to say what you need (whether or not he'll be able to give you what you've asked for); or to negotiate (even though you've never been able to agree on this particular issue before).

It's when you've gone through it all—said the thing that was so hard to say, made the decision that seemed impossible to make, fought the fight you thought could put your whole relationship in jeopardy, expressed the needs you were sure would never be filled— that you can finally bring yourself to the deliverance point. Mystically, amazingly, sometimes after you've given up even believing that such a place could exist, you reach a resolution that seemed impossible only moments before.

Getting there takes courage and practice and will. But it's worth it. Start now by telling yourself that there is such a place—it's a real destination—and then do whatever it takes, no matter what hurdles you have to jump or walls you have to walk through, until, victorious, relieved, transformed, you arrive ... at the deliverance point.

Expose Your Secret Love Scenario

Each of us has a private love scenario, a fantasy about what would make us feel really loved. It represents the fulfillment of our heart's desire, the things we believe could never occur but in our heart of hearts hope will happen anyway. Whatever its magical components, it's often so secret that we haven't even consciously identified it for ourselves.

Exposing your secret scenario is letting yourself and the person you love know exactly the thing, or things, that would make you feel loved and special, whether that's an object (the monogrammed golf clubs), an attitude (an endless array of adoring words), an atmosphere (the exact kind of music), or a sensual preference (the precise way you would like to make love).

It may include the dream of a particular occasion, or may refer to a lifestyle, a special set of circumstances, or an emotional way of being: "What would make me feel really loved is if the woman in my life would sleep all night with her head on my chest. Every night"; "I want a lawn party for my birthday—white dresses, lanterns in the trees, a dance band playing Count Basie songs in the background"; I've always wanted a woman who would sit in the stands while I play polo"; "I've always wanted to go to Paris with someone I love."

Whatever your personal particulars are, the person who loves you needs to know them. Our fantasies can't always be fulfilled, but the chances of having them come true immediately drop to zero if we don't speak up about what they are.

Allowing yourself to discover your scenario and taking the risk of revealing it is the first step in making it come true. For when the person who loves you begins to know your heart's desire, then he or she can start to make it happen. Perhaps he can't afford all those roses right now, but he can give you the first dozen now and remember to bring you the rest when he's flush. So give him a chance. Tell your lover, exactly, precisely, and often just it is that makes you feel loved.

5

*Lifting Your Relationship
to a Higher Level*

Reframe Your Relationship

here are times when we all come to terrible impasses in our relationships—fights we have over and over again, stubborn character flaws that just won't budge, irritating habits that can almost drive us crazy. When we sit in the midst of these things, we can feel angry, bitter, and stuck. In our minds we recite the ways we've been wronged, how terrible he or she's been, how hopeless our relationship is.

The truth is that we've all been wronged; and seemingly unbearable things do happen. There are issues in our relationships that we do go 'round and 'round about, and no matter how much we "work on," negotiate, talk about, or attempt to solve them, we don't seem to make much progress.

At such times, you can feel really discouraged or you can look at your relationship through a different lens.Instead of seeing it as existing to satisfy your every whim, you can lift it up to the spiritual level and ask yourself what it is that you're being invited to learn. If you thought of the problem as a lesson, what would it have to teach you? If you thought of it as a divinely ordained detour, what might it be saving you from? If you construed it to be an invitation to grow in some new direction, what would that be? By lifting it up to the spiritual level, you can begin to see everything that occurs in your relationship as an opportunity for spiritual growth.

That's because whatever is happening in a relationship is happening simultaneously on emotional and spiritual levels. When you view it only on the psychological level, you can keep going around and around in a rat's nest of unresolved problems. But when you lift it up to the spiritual level, let it ascend to where the bright light of truth can shine in, you will, I assure you, see something quite different. There, instead of focusing on the nuisance of the moment as this week's edition of the hopeless situation, you will see that every event in your relationship is something that showed up to expand, inform, or refine you. Instead of endlessly blaming yourself—or your beloved—for the difficulties that inevitably transpire, you will see them as serving a higher purpose—the development of your soul.

When you move to the spiritual level, you recognize lessons, instead of blaming for errors and mistakes. You see your partner no longer as the person who has failed to fulfill all your hopes and dreams, but instead as the person whose spiritual task it has been to embody the very frustrations through which (by struggling and chafing against them) you have developed spiritual maturity. This will also ease you on the emotional level, for when you can feel compassion instead of judgment—for yourself and for your beloved—your relationships will become instantly sweeter, deeper, and more gracious.

See Your Relationships as Part
of the Infinite Love

There are many ways we experience love in our lives—the love of duty, as a man to his country; of pleasure, as in the flower of friendship; of passion and ecstasy, as in romance; or of commitment, as in all the changing vicissitudes of our intimate relationships. And all these are faces, miniature and particular embodiments, of the faceless, infinitely graceful, endlessly tenderhearted Love that is the energy through which we all live and breathe.

In fact, all the love we need and know and seek and make is just a postcard from the landscape of infinite Love. We can discover our connection to that endless and boundless love through particular exalted moments of love in our own lives, like when we fall in love or when a child is born. And, if we are willing to throw our hearts wide open at such moments, we suddenly comprehend that we ourselves are not only participants but the authors of that love. It is then that our human relationships become radiant and illumined, the sacred chalice from which we can sip of the love that is truly divine.

Lie in the Rose Petals

Wouldn't it be wonderful if you could just say, "Come lie with me in the rose petals"—if you had the rose petals to lie in, if you had enough time to lie down in them, if you had the beautiful imagination to whisper such words in the first place.

To be able to say such words would mean that some wonderful things had already happened to you—that your spirit was already free, that your heart was open and clear, that you had already been touched so deeply, so dearly, by someone that you could want to lie down in a bed of rose petals with him, with her, that you have arranged your life, your day, your way of being so that, in fact, you could partake of your own wise and wild invitation.

To say, "Come lie with me in the rose petals" would mean that you have the courage to ask, to risk, to be foolish, to hope and expect, to want, and to wildly imagine, to magically dream. Remember: there is no time like this moment. There are no words more special than the ones you feel moved to utter, no risk more worthy than the one you fancy taking, to move you farther, more deeply, into the sweet bliss of love.

Recognize the Longings of Your Spirit

We are spirits, visitors, explorers here on earth, who have stepped into life in human costume. We are here because we choose to be, because we wouldn't have missed it for the world, because life is a gift—and so very beautiful.

But as spirits we're also a little bit sad, ambivalent about the obligations of this life and of the material world. That's because the spirit is free. It has no substance or contents, no projects or objects. Its essence is pure essence; its purpose is pure being. When spirit engages with matter and we become human beings, our souls still hold the memory of what it was to live in absolute freedom, before the confines of embodiment, intellect, and personality restricted our timeless, radiant essence.

This is why we always carry deep within us the longing for a nameless something, a way, a place, and a grace of living that seem endlessly to elude us. Like a dream whose images vanish just before waking, like the passion whose most exquisite moments cannot be kept and crystallized, like the sound of distant music, we ever so evanescently remember the life of pure spirit we lived before we were born.

It is this remembering that makes us sometimes feel sad about being merely human. We love the beautiful things of this world, but they never quite fill our spirits. Our bodies are magnificent: they bring us the great joys of passion, but they fall away like a husk at the end; we know that they are not us, that we are not them. We fill our lives with the familiar human undertakings—careers, achievements, professions—and our clever, ingenious creations—works of art, music of every sort and order, dancing—and our spirits are moved ... remembering ... yet not quite made ecstatic by what we have said and done.

This niggling but ongoing dissatisfaction we constantly feel with life, no matter how fine and grand it may seem or how beautifully we may have constructed it, is the sign of our true essence. For we are of spirit. And spirit is boundless, a breath in the vast white wind of the infinite soul. Our discontent is its whisper, calling us back to the real beyond real, reminding us where we came from, enticing us back home.

Discover Love in Changing Roles

In the process we once called women's liberation, women fought to make a place for themselves in "the man's world," and this long grueling push toward equality has brought a certain amount of what we might call male power. Even if women still don't hold equal positions in the highest echelons of society, it is true that as a society our attitudes about women have changed. We now believe that women deserve to be equals, whether or not we always grant equality to them. At every level, women have infiltrated the traditionally male-dominated world.

Unfortunately, in the process, neither men nor women have figured out how men can live in relation to all these changes. And as far as men are concerned, they're still trying to redefine themselves in these radically altered circumstances and wondering: What does it mean to have a woman as your boss? What does it mean to have your wife make more money than you do? What does it mean to be a "sensitive" man?

These changes have taxed both men and women in the arena of intimate relationships. What do you need to say to your partner about some issue that is exactly related to the changing roles of women? What do you need to ask for? What do you miss?

For Men: Create a More Intimate Identity

*M*en have always identified themselves in terms of their work. Much more than a woman, a man is what he does. It is the business he runs, the job he holds, and the craft he practices that gives him his sense of identity.

This definition-by-work has been a blessing to both men and women. It has told a man, the woman he loves, and his family, without need for much elaboration, how he spends his time, where his interests lie, and what's important to him. For men and women too, it's a great relief for a man to have a clearly defined identity. Without much effort, a man's work tells everyone who he is. It allows a man to interact with others as a certain identifiable quantity, while at the same time granting him protection from emotional vulnerability.

This is how it's worked in the past—a man was what he did. But now, both men and women want more. What else would you like your partner to know about you beside what you do for a living? What are you proud of? Sharing this kind of information from your far more personal self is what creates a sense of intimacy. Take a step toward more intimacy today.

For Women: Open Your Heart to Men's Pain

*I*dentity through work has been so intrinsic to being a man that even women assume that work will give a man a sense of himself and fulfill his creative impulses. But women are often unaware that men's careers don't necessarily represent the fulfillment of their dreams. Because women have felt so defeated by the economically insulting aspects of what has been traditionally termed women's work, they sometimes assume that men's careers have been the fulfillment of all their desires. But for many men, work has been the life-long disappointment of their hopes, and also a violation of their spirits.

A lot of women have just never considered that setting aside his life dreams could represent a devastating disappointment to a man. Have you ever talked to the man in your life about what he dreamed of being? How could you and he support him now in fulfilling his dreams? Are you willing to explore this with him?

For Women: Encourage the Emotional Exchange

*M*any women are absolutely convinced about the unfeeling nature of men. Their ideas run the gamut from "he couldn't have an emotional life if he tried" to "I can't believe he has a caring bone in his body." These notions cause many women to evaluate all male behavior according to female stereotypes. Instead of reading each man as an individual, let alone perceiving his particular emotional nuances (the feelings under his words, for example), women frequently dismiss men as being emotionally incompetent, and this stereotypical thinking does nothing but exaggerate the problem.

Although women don't come right out and say this, they often act as if they believe it. They keep having their significant emotional relationships with other women, as if they believe that men are emotional novices or incompetents. Since women are familiar with the emotional intensity they can experience with other women, anything that doesn't come up to this level doesn't register on a woman's chart of what a real emotional experience should be. Since women know they can have a great emotional encounter with other women, they often don't even try to create something half or even a quarter as good as that with a man.

But this preference of women for each other's emotional company doesn't do much for our intimate relationships. With men watching Monday Night Football while their wives are talking to each other on the phone, men and women aren't getting any closer. Since women are so good at giving each other an emotional response, their emotional capacity continues to be developed, while men hang around in the background avoiding a deeper emotional connection.

Since men rarely get the kind of positive responses that would encourage them to develop their emotional behavior, they appear to be incapable of developing emotionally. That's why women continue to have their emotional relationships with other women, and we've all become virtually resigned to the fact that this kind of rich emotional exchange can't happen between men and women.

As long as women believe that men can't express their feelings (and therefore don't give men a chance to practice), women perpetuate the frustrating status quo, and in effect keep shutting off the chance to have a wonderful emotional exchange with men.

Today, take a moment to ask a man in your life a personal question and listen, really listen, when he answers. What did you learn? What might you ask and how could you respond next time?

Celebrate a Woman's Strength

*M*any women believe that if they are strong they'll be alone and that if they can give themselves the things that men have always given them—financial and physical security, for example—that men won't want them. Until recently, a lot of what men have had to offer women was their money and protection. When a man can't offer a woman these things, he may sometimes wonder what a strong woman could want or need from him. So, women's fear of being alone if they're strong and self-sufficient isn't just a paranoid fantasy, because it's true that to the degree a woman can provide for herself in any area, she does rob a man of an opportunity to live out part of his familiar identity. And this is uncomfortable for many men.

Intuitively, both men and women know this. That's why some women are afraid of becoming too strong. It's also why some men avoid the women who are. But as women come into their own there's also a lovely opportunity here, for it is precisely the degree that women can become responsible for themselves that men will be relieved of some heavy burdens and freed to find new ways of expressing their connection. While taking on masculine roles can bring women face to face with some very unsettling fears, it can also, paradoxically, deliver them to the possibility of receiving their greatest reward; relationships based not just on survival or economic necessity, but on a completely new level of emotional interchange.

Consecrate the Material

$\mathcal{E}$arly in our relationships, we intuitively know the sacred meaning of objects. The gifts we bring are shining tokens of love; the wedding rings we exchange are material symbols of sacred commitment. But all too often, as time goes on, possessions become an end in themselves. We want things. They're important to us. And rather than being instruments that serve in the cause of love, objects and their acquisition can become the focus of a relationship.

It's not that we don't need possessions, don't need our houses, cars, and stereos. But a home, no matter how humble, can also be a place that truly nurtures your spirit. Indeed, you can decorate your house, choose a given piece of furniture or of art, or select a sound system and music to create the physical environment that will support—rather than take the place of—your deeply felt love.

Instead of wanting and having more and more things, ask yourself what things you have and which you might acquire that will really give you real joy; what objects create a feeling of serenity for you, of inspiration, of happiness? Will it please you to see a vase of flowers on the table or would you prefer the serenity of emptiness?

Your environment is your sanctuary. Allow it to be such. Not all of us can afford the expensive things we might want, but we can all hold our objects in a sacred way. Choose your possessions with care, insist that they serve you in spirit, and ask that they stand as a reflection of the love that is the highest focus of your lives.

Reach for a Spiritual Relationship

To have a spiritual relationship is to consciously acknowledge that above all we are spiritual beings and that the process of our spiritual refinement is our one true undertaking in this life. When you have a spiritual relationship, you choose to embody this truth in love. You shift context and focus. Whereas an emotional relationship has as its focus the contents of the relationship itself, a spiritual relationship sees the spirit's well-being and the soul's journey as its overriding undertakings. Whereas the romantic relationship operates in time, the spiritual union has timeless infinity as its context. Rather than framing itself in life on Earth, it knows that we are all far more than we appear to be, and it joyfully claims as its territory a cosmos that radiates and scintillates, that includes an infinity of angels, and all the stunning coincidental events that are the mysterious instruments of God.

When you love one another in spirit, along with loving, desiring, cherishing, adoring, and protecting your beloved, you will also be the champion of your beloved's spiritual well-being, ensuring that she will make the choices that will allow for her soul's evolution. This may mean creating a quiet environment in which your spirits can flourish, or doing those things—meditating, praying, throwing away the television set—that will encourage a reunion of your souls.

To have an intimate relationship that is also spiritual defies our ordinary Western thinking, for, in a spiritual relationship, we are not seeking the satisfactions of the ego in a conventional way. Instead, we are aware that we are spirits and that we are on the spirit's journey.

The spiritual relationship is gracious, easy, considerate, and kind. Because it has stepped off the merry-go-round of ego concerns, it can be generous and patient, can behold the beloved not just as a person doing this or that, but as a soul on a journey. A great spiritual love does not exclude the psychological and physical—partners will always support each other in these realms with healing and attention—but when you love in the spirit, your love will also be a reminder of the infinite context, the true destination. Remembering this will give your love an exalted, crystalline, and truly luminous quality. For if your emotional relationship is a jewel, your spiritual relationship is the light that shines through it.

Live Your Emotional Healing

*L*ife is a healing journey through which we are moving from a state of forgetfulness about the true nature of our divine being and into a state of remembering and total illumination. Emotional healing is a radical transformation of emotional wounds that results in the revivification of your body, the nourishment of your mind, and, ultimately, the illumination of your soul. It is because our emotions are the arena in which we can so often get derailed in this process that it is of such great importance that we seek our emotional healing. Since, in Western culture, we've been taught so much to perceive ourselves as emotional beings, we tend to stay focused on our emotional vicissitudes; and so long as we have unresolved conflicts on the emotional level, they will stand in the way of our moving on to the higher spiritual levels of love.

Sometimes we seem to be operating on the principle that everyone else was born perfect, and it's only a cruel quirk of fate that, unlike everyone else (who's still perfect), you've still got some ugly knots to untie. Not so. What is true is that within the basic perfection of the gift of life, we're all given certain difficulties, limitations, and problems as a kind of meditative theme to unravel throughout our lives.

Whatever you need to heal—immobilizing fear, explosive rages, abandonment in one or a hundred forms—is grist for transformation, opportunity for enlightenment. For, each time you encounter one of these devastating limitations, you are invited to move through it and, once having healed it, to connect with a higher level of consciousness. On your journey, for example, you may be asked to expand your emotional repertoire from passivity to rage, from rage to forgiveness, from forgiveness to compassion, and from compassion to indivisible love.

Because love is our ultimate destination, this journey of healing is your life's true work. It doesn't matter whether you undertake it with additional help from psychotherapy, meditation, tai chi, weight lifting, Alcoholics Anonymous, the Baptist Church, vegetarianism, or an intimate relationship. Any path to healing, devotedly pursued, can deliver you to this destination—for there is no other. What does make a difference is whether or not you take the journey. If you don't, you will live awash in self-pity, endlessly tossed by your feelings, your unfinished emotional business. But if you do, you will see that what started out as your painful limitations became in the end your most radiant assets; and your soul, released at last from its endless emotional involvements, will emerge as the shining envoy of your love.

Pursue Beauty

Beauty is luminous radiance. Beauty is lucent, mystical essence, the face that is unforgettably lovely, the dance with the exquisite movements that our minds cannot erase, the music whose notes repeat themselves endlessly in our hearts. Beauty infuses; beauty enthralls; beauty inspires and illumines; beauty lifts up and enlivens our souls.

Beauty applies to both the material and the ethereal worlds. Beauty calls on our organs of perception (she's a beautiful woman) as well as our spiritual sensitivity (it was a beautiful experience) and mystically coordinates these worlds for us. Whereas beauty is embodied in form, the apprehension of beauty, whatever its form, is an experience of transcendence. It is this remarkable capacity of beauty to be at once both immanent and transcendent that causes us to pursue it, to be moved by it, and to recognize that in some ineffable way we can trust it as the measure of what has value for our souls.

Beauty also enchants us because its essence is to embody more, a higher level of whatever it is that we are perceiving. In standing above all others, the beautiful thing invites everything around it to rise to its own level. So it is that the beautiful moment teases us to make all moments beautiful, the beauty of the written word to elevate our own language, the sound of beautiful music to surrender to the beautiful soundless stillness in our own hearts.

Fill your life with beauty. Allow your beauty to shimmer forth. Anoint your house with beautiful things: objects, fragrances, movements, moments, sounds, emotions. Beautiful food is a sanctification of the body. Beautiful ideas are a feast for the mind. Beautiful art and music are a banquet for soul. We must seek beauty, respond to it, cultivate it, and surround ourselves with it, for beauty in this life is a reflection of our souls, as our souls shall be forever a pure reflection of it.

Let Go, Surrender

When in doubt, let go—give way; give in. When in expectation, frustration, or pain; when in confusion, impatience, or fear; when you don't know what to do next; when you're losing control— let go. Let go. Give up. Give in.

Letting go is emotional and spiritual surrender. It means willingly jumping out of the lifeboat of your preconceptions of reality and taking your chances out in the open sea of anything-can-happen. It means that even as your definition of reality is dissolving before your very eyes, you willingly relinquish it, instinctively comprehending that the state of surrender itself will be a creative condition.

It's hard to let go, to live in the formless, destinationless place. All our lives we're taught to hold on, to be the masters of our fate, the captains of our soul. Letting go isn't comfortable; it can feel like anything from laziness to utter loss of control. It's not aggressive and self-assured. It's not the American way.

But letting go is, in truth, a most elegant kind of daring. It is vulnerability of the highest order, an emptying out of the self, of all the clutter and chatter that, ordinarily, we all contain—ideas, attitudes, schemes, and plans—and offering your self as an empty vessel to be filled. In this emptiness there is room for so much; in this vacancy, anything can happen: breathtaking transformations, changes of direction, miracles that will purely astound you, love that comes out of the woodwork, spiritual conversion . . . But only if you are willing to truly let go of it all: as the tree dropping her bright leaves for winter, the trapeze artist, suspended in midair between the two bars, the diver free-falling from the high-dive—have all unequivocally, wholeheartedly let go.

Letting go is being alive to the power of the nothingness. It is living in surrender, trust, and the belief that emptiness is at once the perfect completion and the perfect beginning. So let go. And remember that should you hang on to even a shred, or try to make a deal with the gods ("I'll let go, but only if . . .") then nothing new—or wonderful—can happen.

Respect the Opposite Sex

t is certainly sad and seems almost strange that we actually have to encourage ourselves to respect the opposite sex. But unfortunately, because for decades we've been bombarded with articles and books that underline the differences between men and women, we now live in a world in which we're surrounded by antagonism between the sexes. For the sake of our relationships, we really must consciously choose to honor the opposite sex.

Honoring means remembering the value of, cherishing, holding dear, celebrating rather than disparaging the differences between, and savoring the blessings of the other. It means not building walls out of differences, but delighting in each beautiful amusing one, seeing it as the counterpart and balance to your own splendid and hilarious uniqueness.

As you honor the opposite sex, you'll start moving from the surface to the depths, realizing that beneath the familiar costumes of gender we all embody a similar evolving consciousness, that inside we all carry as a great emotional treasure the same exquisite array of feelings. A man's grief over the death of his father is no less real than a woman's grief over the loss of hers. A man's heart will be as poignantly, beautifully touched by a breathtaking sunset, the rustle of cottonwood leaves in Yosemite, or a cool, crystalline autumn morning as a woman's. At the core we are all moved by our sorrows and by the magnificence and miracles that touch us, not as men or women, but as human beings.

To know this is to relax the wearying focus on our differences, to come graciously into the knowing that we can honor one another without harming or shortchanging ourselves. Take a moment today to remember that what we live and suffer, we live and suffer in common, and that real love, love in the soul, is beyond male and female, beyond gender as an issue at all.

Be Graceful, Hopeful, and Wise

*G*race is beauty of the spirit. Hope is the optimism of the soul, and wisdom is the soul's intelligence. These all are qualities of such eloquence that even as we hear the words, a quiet settles in our beings, as if from a far distant place we have heard once again the names of the elegant ancient virtues: Grace. Hope. Wisdom.

Grace, hope, and wisdom are all qualities of the soul. They refer to how our spirits operate in the world; they call up a sense of our deeper engagement with reality, and tell us again that, over, around, and through everything, a beautiful spiritual consciousness is quietly operating. So it is that grace adds a quality of silkiness to all our movements, not only the way we move with our bodies, but the way our spirits inhabit them; not only the way we move through the world, but the way in which, because of our genteel openness, we allow the world to move through us. Grace is beauty, refinement of the spirit. We feel it, recognize it, are beautifully softened and engaged by it, whenever we stand in its presence. In bringing us into its comeliness, grace brings us into our depth. We hold it as the measure of what we may longingly aspire to as the spiritual grandeur in our lives.

Hope is promise. When the present seems unbearable, hope allows us to live in the future and, there, to find ease. When we hope, we partake of the state of absolute calm that has already understood that everything we have done and everything we shall do, will be beautiful somewhere, sometime; that our sorrows will enhance us, that even our tragedies will bring us to our depth.

In wisdom we know without learning; we comprehend without effort. We remember what we were never told and can offer it, graciously, easily, as the truth that heals, the observation that clarifies, the intuition that illumines and brilliantly transforms. Wisdom is the soul's intelligence delivered, shared—the soul's ancient knowledge unself-consciously revealed—in words that ring with the truth we have always known but never before been able to fully perceive.

Grace makes life fluid, flowing, and fine. Hope makes life lucky, exquisitely foreseen. And wisdom allows us to know when to trust grace and hope. Grace, wisdom, and hope are not shiny little virtues, but grand powers of the soul that will insist through their stunning magnificence that everything else in your life rise up to meet them.

Celebrate the Power of Your Union

It is because in the "we" of union that the individual "I" can become ever more beautifully developed that we enter into relationships in the first place. Somewhere, intuitively, we all know that love will make more of us than we ever would have become on our own. So without so much as a breathtaking pause, we "fall in love," give ourselves over to the charms of our beloved, and surrender ourselves to the mysteries of union.

Here everything changes. Through each nuance of behavior, whether a kiss, a conversation, the income taxes, or making love, you are asked to take account not only of your beloved, but also of your relationship. That's because when you fall in love, there's another spiritual entity—the "we," the "us"—that is brought into being. Although it's invisible, it is utterly alive—vibrant, vivid, and unique; continuously present as a discrete though subtle energetic essence. You can feel it when you're alone together as the mysterious unified play of your two energies.

This entity, like the individuals in it, must be nourished. When you honor your relationship—by speaking adoringly of it to others, by treating your sexual relationship as a sacred bond, by standing fast together in times of turmoil and sorrow—you strengthen the power of your union. You nourish the "we" as the precious being it is, celebrate the unique, unrepeatable identity it has, and reweave the blanket of love that will warm and protect your union always.

Reach for the Depth, Meaning, and Intimacy

Depth, meaning, and intimacy are not givens in a relationship. They don't just "come with the territory." You can't have them just because you "fall in love," "have a relationship," or "get married." Rather, they are very high qualities for any relationship, qualities that refer to the highest parts of our being, to our spiritual dimension.

When we speak of depth, we are referring to something that has the capacity to move us emotionally to a very high degree. We long for depth because depth shows us our true nature as human beings, dimensions that are not part of the ordinary goings on of daily life. When we encounter our depth, we come into contact with the further reaches of ourselves and we can suddenly understand that life is much grander than we ever imagined. There's a thrill in coming face to face with our own depth, but there's an even greater thrill when we experience depth in a relationship. When you feel deeply connected to the person you love, he or she has joined you in the quality of experience that allows you to see that life is more than just what you're having for dinner or how you're going to pay the bills. Depth gives your life together a quality and richness that simply don't exist without it.

Meaning has to do with the significance of things; in particular, with how things are significant to each of us. Your birthday has meaning, for example, because it reminds you of the miracle of your own life. It makes you feel precious. Similarly, when we experience meaning in a relationship, we suddenly understand that life has qualities and values that are much greater than we imagined. This comforts us; it gives us a sense of ease. Instead of feeling like we're trapped in a random universe where anything can happen and nothing can be counted on, we suddenly understand that life is orderly and beautiful, that it is, in fact, exquisitely designed; we can relax our cares and concerns in the beautiful, carrying basket that meaning provides for us.

Intimacy is that special feeling of closeness that's the bottom line of what we want out of our relationships. It's the feeling of being very connected to someone and it is what makes us feel not only happy to be alive, but happy to be alive in the company of our beloved. Instead of being on a long, struggling, curious journey on our own, we recognize that we have company and that our burdens, as well as our great joys, can be shared. Intimacy is the sharing of all our life experiences, whether deep and meaningful, or casual and everyday. The more you have this exchange, the more connected you will feel to the person you love.

Depth, meaning, and intimacy are all qualities that are a reflection of our souls, that part in each of us which is eternal and precious beyond words. So, as we seek to infuse them into our relationships, we are reaching for something that operates on a spiritual level and gives us the great satisfaction of recognizing that we are spirits as well as mortal human beings. Seen in this way, a relationship is the gift of a lifetime, one to be treasured always.

May you find and nurture the depth, intimacy, and meaning in your own true love.

Recognize the Higher Purpose
of a Relationship

We are all in the beautiful, endlessly unfolding process of our own development. We're not tin soldiers or nutcracker human beings; we are living beings who are a pliable, changeable, fluid, self-creating consciousness that is being formed and reformed as we live our lives through the individuals and circumstances we encounter.

That's why every relationship you have, no matter how short, is purposeful. It is the transformational process of two souls' evolution and mutual psychological healing. To the degree that you're conscious of this deep purpose, you become able both to recognize the love that's right for you and also to receive its benefits.

The truth is that when you call love into your life, you're not just asking for someone who meets your relationship requirements. You're also asking to step into alignment with your life's highest purpose.

That's because whether you are consciously aware of it or not, your life has its own unique purpose and the person who joins you in love is stepping into your life to help you fulfill that purpose. Whether his or her role is great or small in relation to your life's journey, whether he or she joins you by bringing joy or the frustrations that refine and ultimately define you, this person is arriving to help you clarify and fulfill your destiny. The same is true for you vis-à-vis him or her. You have entered that person's life to do the same.

What do you believe your own life's purpose to be? How could a loving partner assist you in fulfilling it? How will being aware of this change what you are seeking in a relationship?

Remember That Love Is a Paradox

True love is paradoxical: Everything you can say about it is both true and not true at the same time. This applies to the nature of love itself—that it is exalted and mundane; that it takes us to limitless joy, but also has limitations; that it fulfills our demands to be loved, yet can totally defy and ignore our specific requirements.

The way this paradox manifests in the real world is that if you insist on something about love, you never get it—or you do. If you insist that it arrives at a certain time, comes in a certain package, lasts a certain length of time, behaves in a certain way, challenges you in exactly all the ways you'd like it to, you'll never get it—or, on the other hand, you'll get exactly what you ordered.

You just never know. That's the paradox of love. As someone said to a dear friend of mine as she stood devastated after the breakup of her fourteen-year-marriage, "Well, maybe now you'll meet the man of your dreams and live happily ever after, or maybe you'll be miserable for the rest of your life." In her case, amazingly, she found the perfect man six months later, but of course there was no guarantee that she would.

The paradoxes embedded in love reveal the great truth that love is always a gift. You can want it, ask for it, pray for it, do spells and chants to call it into your life, and even have faith that it will arrive. But ultimately it's only when you allow yourself to float in the great sea of life, and give up all control, that love can finally show up for you. It may arrive just when you want it, or so long after you've given up that you aren't even sure you want it anymore. You just never know.

Like a Christmas present, it may be exactly the thing you hoped you'd find under the tree—or something you never imagined or dreamed of. The paradox is that, if it really is love, you'll be overjoyed to receive it.

No matter how or when love arrives, the amazing thing is that when it does, it takes over. You can't do anything except jump for joy and throw up your arms and shout, "I'm in love! Can you believe it? I've finally found the love of my life!"

Remember Your Soulful Connection

Since time immemorial, men and women have loved one another—desperately, madly, sweetly, with unbridled, dangerous passion, with the compassion of their kind hearts, to the depth of their souls. Love knows no bounds. There is no country, province, or people to which it has ever been irrelevant; and, whenever you fall in love, you join the company of lovers of all times in living out one of life's greatest themes.

What you feel when you fall in love is universal. However ordinary or simple your own love may appear to be, to your heart and soul it is a grand love. Like David and Bathsheba, Antony and Cleopatra, Romeo and Juliet, Abelard and Heloise, your love, too, is an experience of wonder and ecstatic belonging that will draw you into life's most tragic and beautiful moments. Through love you become part of a sacred tradition, that great lineage of all those who have plighted their troth and chosen to live and die for love.

We need love.

We seek love because in every cell of our being we know that love is the only thing we cannot live without. This is why no matter what else we may do or pursue in our lives, love is always our highest goal, our farthest reach, our most passionate quest. Remembering this, may you seek it, find it, and nourish it so it can always inspire you with its greatest gifts.

Know Each Other Like the Seasons

The journey of love is a journey of many sweet discoveries. In a new love, it's the sweet bliss of discovering all your beloved's little secrets, her favorite flower and fragrance, the color that sets off her eyes; his plaid flannel shirt, the way he laces his boots, his old shaving brush; the scent of her skin, the feel of her hair, the drawer she keeps her lingerie in.

It is, later, the being together of love—the sound of the key as he locks up the house, of the rain in the shower each morning, as, singing, she washes her hair. It is how she rolls over at night in bed, how he sleeps, like a saint, with his hands folded over his chest; it is what he can fix; what she can mend.

And it is the changing, this way and that way. Arguing. There are the bad words, the anger and love in the midst; making love, holding hands. And the children, seeing them sleeping and being carried, at night, in his arms; how he is so tender, how she is so easy, so strong with them.

It is watching the years go. Autumn and spring and winter and summer. So slowly and endlessly beautifully folding, unfolding. And how we have done every year, so many things. And so few. Each day, and the meals and the work and the talk. Each day a small town with a map, and the trip we have taken in it. And the walks and the light, and the changing of the light. And how we have traveled. And how we have given the gifts. At Christmas. On birthdays. And all the words. The cards. The things we have said. The things we have whispered. I love you. Good night. I adore you. You are the one.

Hold Your Beloved in Special Awareness

When you love someone at a soul level, you carry a very special awareness on behalf of that person. In the depths of your being, you have agreed to know, see, sense, and feel for this person with a subtle kind of attention that continually takes the truth of his or her being into account.

The attention we can carry for one another runs the gamut from holding a quiet place in your heart so your beloved can go through his emotional healing to knowing that the person you love needs money, time, or space, even when she isn't consciously aware of it and can't ask you for it directly. Sometimes our refined perception takes the form of "just happening by" at the moment of crisis. At others, it may mean holding the awareness that the person you love has issues about her health, weight, body image, or a particular physical feature, and being sensitive and supportive around that particular issue. You may hold your beloved in your awareness by recognizing that he or she has a deep fear of abandonment to which you can respond by being realistically reassuring, generous, and steadfast in your expressions of love. If your sweetheart has been sexually abused you can consciously encourage him or her to protect his boundaries or seek her emotional healing.

Sometimes we carry this special awareness consciously; at other times it's secret even to us, a brilliant act of intuition that just seems to occur. The man who brings home flowers "for no reason" only to discover that minutes ago his wife received news of her mother's sudden death has unconsciously "sensed" her pain and met her need before she could even express it. Similarly, the woman who "doesn't know why" but shows up at her husband's office with lunch only to find out that earlier that morning his biggest deal of the year fell apart is also acting on an intuition unconscious even to herself.

Rather than expecting your beloved to consciously verbalize every single thing that he or she needs, try to step in at times and recognize the unspoken, addressing it with intuitive kindness and care. Practice your special awareness because this sort of intuitive second-guessing is one of the most precious gifts of love.

Face Your Denials

*D*enial—actively forgetting, not admitting, or not letting yourself know, see, face, or recognize a difficult truth about yourself—is a psychological position that most of us employ to one degree or another. Denial serves emotional and even spiritual functions, and it is always a wall around pain. Denial protects us from the abuse, abandonment, bad examples, and failures of love that are always hard to face head-on. But denial is a half-baked, temporary solution; and its consequences in the long run can be far worse than facing the pain that created it in the first place.

Consistently practiced, denial represents a spiritual compromise, a disability that threatens to limit our growth on every level. It cordons off attributes and behaviors in ourselves, which, so long as we hold them in denial, have the capacity to constrict if not utterly destroy our lives. Thus, the alcoholic in denial runs the risk of crashing her car, going to jail, losing her husband, job, children, social status, soul, and even her life so long as she persists in her denial; and the person who refuses to face his addictive use of credit cards runs similar risks.

Because of its very nature—an unconscious but deeply intentioned not-knowing—it's hard to see your own denials. Doing so requires courage and the expansiveness of spirit that will allow you to face your own negative aspects. If your present lover, an ex-girlfriend, five friends, six strangers, and a few enemies suggest that you have a problem with alcohol, that you're a passive-aggressive manipulator, that the way you handle anger is really off the charts, you'd better summon the courage to take a hard look (with professional help if you need it) at the truth that might lie behind these (admittedly hard to hear) accusations.

It's painful looking behind the curtain of our own denials. There's so much to face—old wounds, the fear that you won't have the strength to go on. Indeed, facing your denials takes courage precisely because it can feel more like an assault on your fragile ego and flimsy self-esteem than a step toward self-improvement.

But these hurdles are part of the process. Ego, and even self-esteem, if we hold them up too high or get too attached to them, can be strongholds of denial in themselves. We get so involved in protecting them, as image, that we forget the real person behind them. The truth is that there's nothing so fine as yourself—you, just as you are, with the feelings you've often been too scared to feel, with the flaws that are charmingly yours, with the sadness and hurt you can bear.

So take courage and face your denials, for behind your denials hides your radiant spirit, a whole, new, conscious self just waiting to face the truth, and to finally be born.

Open to the Ecstatic Energy

*L*ife is breath, movement. As long as you are capable of movement, you inhabit life and the energy of life inhabits you. In this state, every step you take, every word you utter, every thought that passes through the magic electronic circuitry of your brain, every single gesture you enact is an expression of your vivid aliveness, a sign that you are a mortal, alive human being.

Sometimes in our overemphasis on verbal communication, we forget that we are also bodies and that as physical beings, too, we have a unique and powerful language. In our bodies, we "feel" and know things often before we can even begin to articulate them. Through our bodies, we share our love in an immediate, instinctual way that conveys a depth of feeling beyond words.

The language of the body is this energy, the invisible, ecstatic pulse that is the essence of life itself. We often think of our aliveness only as form—the bodies we inhabit—and not as the life force, or energy, that flows through them. In doing so, we miss feeling our own aliveness, and, in relationships, to be nourished by that mysterious spiritual commodity that is another person's "energy." Yet it is precisely the "energy"—of a city, a person, a piece of music, or an emotional exchange—that actually moves us at the deepest level. Nothing reveals this more clearly than a body which, through illness, is being drained of its energetic essence; and nothing demonstrates the presence of energy more dramatically than children.

In our intimate relationships, when we shift our attention from the material form—what we look like, what we're wearing, how in or out of shape we are—and move into the energetic realm, we enter the mystical arena in which we experience love itself as an expression of this energy. Instead of feeling it only as an emotion, we also sense it as an invisible pulse, the heart-filling throb, the luminous shivers that tell our bodies we have truly "felt" our love.

To move your focus from substance to energy and to seek the person whose energy, for you, is ecstatic, is to immediately expand your repertoire of love. When you do, you will not only be able to talk about the love you feel, you will actually be able to "feel" it as the tingling, brilliant, ecstatic presence in your body. So open your heart—and every cell of your being—to the luminous life-changing wisdom that is your soul's ecstatic energy.

Discover Sex as Sacred Reunion

Our sexuality is one of the loveliest, most complex, and satisfying aspects of our intimate relationships. It is where we gather in the flesh to be joined, connected, and bonded. It can bring us joy or disappointment. It can be the source of our most painful betrayals, or of the highest moments of our ecstatic love.

Just as bringing our bodies together in the sexual encounter reminds us that we are bodies, essentially physical beings, so orgasm, the moment of blossoming ecstasy, connects us to the spiritual essence within us. Taken in total, making love is the movement of the mystic, electric current that bears eloquent witness to the fact that we are not just physical beings but temples wherein the spirit resides.

To apprehend your lovemaking in this way is to move toward the sacred in your sexual relationship. It is to ask more of it, give more to it, and receive more, far more, from it than you can ever expect from the how-to-improve-your-sex-life articles in popular magazines. Although handy-dandy advice columns and erotic manuals may indeed solve some of your sexual machinery problems, they will drop you off at the doorway of sex as a gymnasium, romance novel, or power trip, leaving you with only a sensate thrill. Thus you are denied the magnificent opportunity of experiencing your sexual encounters as a spiritual reunion of the highest order.

In making love, it is not only our bodies that are happily and deliciously engaged; but, because of the irresistible magnetism that sexual attraction is, we are also invited to contemplate in the mind and actually experience in the body the spirit which lives and moves within us.

Through sex we enter the timeless, boundary-less moment. We partake of the one experience above all others in life that allows us the bliss of true union. Here ego and all its concerns are erased, and the self is dissolved in utter surrender. To know, feel, and discover this in the presence of another human being, as we are invited to do in making love, is to be brought face to face with one of the greatest mysteries of human existence—that we are spirit, embodied, and that, as human beings, we are partaking in this miracle.

Protect Your Soul

The journey of the soul is not all joy, nor is it always consummated in the light, for in this life we make a choice at every moment of what our soul's destination shall be. Just as in a dance one may move in any direction—forward and sideways, fly beautifully elevated or be bowed down toward the earth—so in life do we also choose a direction, the path our souls will take.

If a man kills his wife and uses the legal system's loopholes to escape conviction, he has not only gotten away with murder, he has lost his soul. He may be set free, return to the usual circumstances of his life, but he will never be free; he will be a soulless man whose very existence is the embodiment of untruth. No matter how many people he may falsely convince of his innocence, in the light of the truth he is still condemned; and should he try insanely to convince himself of his own innocence, then surely his soul shall be lifted by darkness from him.

There is no neutral moment or action in our experience.

Everything we do, every action we enact, every nuance of movement, each word we utter either creates the further illumination of our souls or moves us in a direction in which, in a moment of dark unconsciousness, our souls can be utterly compromised.

The potential for loss of soul—to one degree or another—is the affliction of a society that as a collective has lost its sense of the holy, of a culture that values everything else above the spiritual. We live in such a spiritually impoverished culture—and in such a time. Loss of soul, to one degree or another, is a constant teasing possibility. We are invited at every corner to hedge on the truth, indulge ourselves, act as if our words and actions have no ultimate consequence, make an absolute of the material world, and treat the spiritual world as if it were some kind of frothy, angelic fantasy. In such a world the soul struggles for survival; in such a world a man can lose his own soul and have the whole culture support him, and in such a world, conversely, the light of a single, great soul that lives in integrity can truly illumine the world.

Sanctify Your Relationship

Whether it is clearly visible or not, every relationship has a higher purpose than itself alone, a meaning that goes beyond the conventions of love and romance. This purpose shapes us individually and changes, if only in some small way, the essential nature of the reality we have entered here by being born.

Once you know this you will recognize that whatever occurs between you—both the petty dramas and the life-shaping tragedies—are part of a larger plan, that they are honing you for your unique participation in the human experience. You will also accept that the person you love has come into your life for a reason that goes beyond the satisfactions of the moment or even your personal future to reach into the web of time beyond time.

What you do here together, how well and how beautifully you do it, has implications not only for how cozily you will sit together in your rocking chairs in your old age, but also for every other living being. That's because we are all participants in the process of creating a species and a world that hums with peace and is informed by love. This is our highest purpose, and when we sanctify our relationships, the difficulties they contain will be instantly diminished and what will stand in their place is the overwhelming presence of real love.

Recognizing that your relationship is purposeful means seeing it not as an act of self-indulgence, but rather as an offering of love that together you are giving to the world.

Consecrate Your Relationship

Personal rituals provide a reference not only for the value we place upon whatever we are consecrating, but also for the value we ask be conferred upon them. We consecrate our relationships when we set them apart from the ordinary through ritual.

When I was a child, my father would always say a prayer before dinner on my birthday: "With thanksgiving and love that you have been given to be a part of our hearts and of our family, we celebrate this day of your birth, beautiful child, delightful spirit. May you have a year full of joy and may your prodigious talents, like arrows, find their true mark through a long life in this world."

In the presence of these consecrating words, my life became more than simply the life I was leading. It became a holy place, with qualities and possibilities. It became a privilege and a responsibility. No matter what difficult times I came to, no matter what hardships I faced, the ritual of these consecrated words was a beautiful reference that pointed me to my higher purpose.

Relationships, too, can be consecrated in this way, made holy by the rituals and ceremonies that, in their mystical capacity, have the power to set them apart. Ceremonies say, in effect, this day is not like all other days, this person is not like all other people; this love is not like all other loves.

While you may think of consecration as something that can only happen in a church, the truth is that we all have the capacity to hallow our relationships. The consecration of your relationship is a creative and deeply private affair. Set aside a special time to acknowledge your union—your wedding or partnership anniversary perhaps. Designate a specific place in which to honor it; and create your own private ceremony. Light candles, say words, play music.

Consecrating your relationship is the sign that you view your relationship as holy, and that you intend, through it and with your beloved as your witness, always to live it to its highest purpose.

Bow to the Mystery of Love

A relationship—two people coming together to live, to work, to play, to laugh, to grieve, to rejoice, to make love—is the form that human beings give to love, but love itself, that ineffable essence that draws us together into communion with one another, is beyond definition, beyond analysis. Love has its own way. Love just is.

Love is a mystery, the essence of which is angelic. In its very nature it goes beyond what we can understand by any of the systems through which we usually comprehend reality. It exists simultaneously outside us and within us. It both binds and frees us. It opens our hearts and breaks our hearts. It cannot be seen, except in the eyes of the beloved, nor felt except in the heart of the one who is cherished. Invisible, its absence leaves us gray-hearted, wounded in spirit, while its presence transforms our hearts, our psyches, and our lives.

We seek love, without knowing what it is, knowing we will know when we find it. This is the true mystery of love—that no matter how much we are unable to describe it, we always recognize it when we experience it.

In bowing to the mystery of love we acknowledge that love is beyond our comprehension, that we will never fully understand it. The love we seek seeks us, embraces us without our knowing, and binds our spirits into the body of itself. There is a point at which in the presence of love there is nothing more to say or prove, nothing left to ask for or regret, nothing left except the miracle of love itself.

About the Author

*D*aphne Rose Kingma is a psychotherapist who has counseled couples and individuals to a deeper understanding and improvement of their relationships for more than 25 years. She has been a frequent guest on *Oprah* and is the best-selling author of many books including *True Love, Finding True Love,* and *Loving Yourself.* She lives in Santa Barbara, California.

For lectures, workshops or comments, you can reach her at *daphnekingma.com.*

To Our Readers

*C*onari Press, an imprint of Red Wheel/Weiser, publishes books on topics ranging from spirituality, personal growth, and relationships to women's issues, parenting, and social issues. Our mission is to publish quality books that will make a difference in people's lives— how we feel about ourselves and how we relate to one another. We value integrity, compassion, and receptivity, both in the books we publish and in the way we do business.

Our readers are our most important resource, and we value your input, suggestions, and ideas about what you would like to see published. Please feel free to contact us, to request our latest book catalog, or to be added to our mailing list.

Conari Press
An imprint of Red Wheel/Weiser, LLC
P.O. Box 612
York Beach, ME 03910-0612
www.conari.com